Spiritual
Wonderings
& Wanderings

Inspirational Reflections
on the Catholic Church & Culture

Rev. Joe Jagodensky, SDS.

a Roman Catholic priest and member
of the Society of the Divine Savior (Salvatorians)
www.Salvatorians.com

Also available on Amazon is
"Soulful Musings," reflections on Church & Culture and
"Living Life's Mysteries," Seasonal Christian Reflections -
Advent, Christmas, Lent and Easter

"As If"

Act As If. .

Pretending is for children.Grown-ups don't have the time or interest to imagine what could be, either for their families or for the world. Instead of perceiving it as pretending perhaps the words "as if" could be included in the sentence. Maybe that would help us.

What is we act "as if" we are a people at peace and people who can cooperate and dialogue together, treat each other "as if" we care what happens to them - even clerks and store employees. A smile, a nod, a friendly exchange about the weather or the current holiday. If our "as if's" occurred more often, then perhaps "will be" can slowly come about.

I had two childhood dreams. (This is the pretending part.) I wanted to be in radio and become a priest. As time progressed, I acted "as if" I were a radio announcer and were a priest. I created an imitation radio program while in 8th grade and also had a fake mass, complete with vestments, linens and chalices. It was "as if" I was a radio announcer and a priest.

I was able to achieve both dreams. Some people may call it destiny or a habit that become real. I like to think of it as two simple pretending dreams of acting "as if." How does a priest act? I would attempt to duplicate those actions. How does a radio announcer sound? I would try to imitate that voice, inflection or cadence of a radio announcer.

It was "as if" I were something that I was yet not. Yet, perhaps I was those careers and pretending prepared me for those real experiences. "As if." Can we act "as if" the world was at peace or that peace is at least possible? Can we pretend, like a child with our "as if's" but with an adult's view?

I guess you can take this just so far. But what a great phrase, "...it's as if I..."

"Topsy Turvy"

This is a little known theological concept that you may feel free to use in conversations, especially when there's a lull. Impress your friends when you tell them that "Jesus had this, how shall I put it, a 'topsy turvy' mission." The silence will immediately begin and then comes the difficult part. How do you explain what this concept means?

St. Augustine can help us out when he writes,

"The bread might be hungry, and the fountain thirsty
That the light might sleep, and the way be weary from the journey
That the truth might be accused by false witnesses, and the judge of the living and dead be judged by a mortal judge
That justice might be convicted by the unjust and discipline be scourged with whips
That the cluster of grapes might be crowned with thorns, and the foundation be hung on a tree
That strength might grow weak, eternal health be wounded, life die
That the one who was born of the Father, not made by the Father, was made in the Mother whom he had made; so
That he might exist here for a time, being born of her who could never and nowhere have existed except through him."

That's "Topsy Turvy."
Have a great conversation with your friends
but don't let them off the hock with easy, negative replies.

Enlarged Heart? It's a Good Thing

Medicine has all kinds of maladies concerning the heart. Heart attack? Call 911. Enlarged heart? Drugs for the rest of your life.

Those medical alerts are conversely spiritual gifts. A heart attack in spirituality is called passion and a deep love that is enveloping, it jolts our pumping organ. An enlarged heart? What better definition for spirituality than to have a diagnosis of an "enlarged heart." To be afflicted with an enlarged heart means that you have opened yourself up to something or someone greater than yourself and by doing so, the graces that flow to and from you are huge. Having an enlarged heart is so much better than the petty little ones that pump just enough blood to keep up with jealousy, competition, paranoia and selfishness our minds produce. An enlarged heart has room for so much more and for so many more.

We look at others to see how we can improve our lives. We model for others and we look for models. In medicine it is called "contagious." Scary word with even scarier consequences. Spiritually, "contagion" of God's heart is a wonderful and inviting event. It becomes infectious. (Another bad medical word but a spiritually cherished one.)

Let us infect each other with enlarged hearts that break down divisions that are so common. Find a common ground with someone who disagrees with you on most issues and build from there to share enough to make your hearts "enlarged."

Strengthen your heart with a heart attack of love, compassion, mercy,

The Silence of St. Joseph

Lot's wife has no name, the thousands fed with mere fish and bread doesn't include women and children and Joseph says nothing in the Bible. The next cocktail party you attend, you can amaze your friends with these tiny bits of trivia.

God speaks to Joseph through dreams. He was aware of them, interpreted them and acted upon them. Lucky for the Holy Family. He probably learned more in his silence than in telling everyone what to think or what was good or bad in the world. Joseph's silence opened him up to hear the voice of God, in his case, found in dreams.

A fellow employee told me that when she arrives home, the television goes on and stays on. Imagine all those TV ads floating around somewhere in her head every night. (No wonder I thought she was hyper at work.) She had no silence. There wasn't room in her head for anything other than toilet cleaners, divorce attorneys and cheap car insurance.

Winter has its drawbacks but it holds for me one beautiful benefit. The doors and windows are closed as the cold wants to whisk its way in and there is a new found silence that fills the house. A quiet that can either be boredom or blessed.

Our culture prides itself on noise and lights. You can't get away from it. Without our knowing it, the toll it must take on our psyche and soul must be astounding. Studies are showing how "Facebook" and other social media can consume our dopamine lives.

I was about to say why not "take some time out for silence" but that sounds too cheesy. You don't take "time out" or you just end up sitting there wondering when this scheduled time of silence will end. A space needs to be created within you that allows silence to fill you up in order to shut you down.

Joseph's silence was blessed and graced. It provided insight that no one else knew from marrying a pregnant Mary to enabling his family to escape death. A true benefit from winter's noisy weather.

"Forever"

I love satellite radio. Since sliced bread, I can't think of anything comparable. Commercial free, varied and so many musical and informational offerings. I renew it every three years. Easy to remember. My renewal came up so I called to renew for another three years and the operator said, "For an additional $60.00 you can have it forever?" I was stumped but amused.

Do I choose "forever" or "three years." The decisions we must make in life. I paused and said, "Is satellite going out of business?" The operator laughed and assured me that no, it's here to stay. I'm thinking what does "forever" mean in business anyway. My hardware store will be here forever? My pharmacy store will be beside me forever (and as Catholics add another "ever")?

I bought her "forever" extra charge and I need never make another payment for the rest of my life. Am I stupid? Frugal? Wishful?

I have a wedding ceremony soon and thought I'd talk about that word "forever." I could talk forever at the wedding but thought it best to contain it. What does "forever" mean in marriage?

In our U.S. culture, I don't think I'd make a Vegas bet. A $20,000.00 wedding ceremony and the bets are on five married years, tops. We're too influenced by others to decide otherwise. It's too convenient to get out of a marriage these days. (I love the ads for "Christian divorce attorneys" who swear that there's a calm, civilized way of divorcing. I think that contradicts what divorce is. It should be divisive and hurtful. Otherwise, why do it? Also, what's "calm and civilized" about Christianity?)

The Catholic Church ends many prayers with the words "forever and ever." Whenever you want Catholics to respond just say, "Forever and ever." Instant reply. Is it overkill? I think so. "Forever" isn't enough that the Church needs to add another "ever" after it? (Will this marriage ever end?!)

Ironically, "forever" means now. What are you doing now? What are you thinking now? Our nows make forevers happen.

So I'm enjoying my satellite radio.... for now.

Yes

I hate when someone calls to ask a favor and begins with the question, "What are doing tomorrow night?" I have no idea what is involved but I'm expected to give an instant answer. I say, "Yes," and then I hear, "Oh good, you can help me clean the bathroom." Now I'm stuck. Instead of being asked, "Would you like to come to supper tomorrow night?" Then I know what's expected and can either lie or accept.

God, of course, is the one asking the first question and we are expected to reply, "Yes," always without knowing the request. "Are you willing to live life?" God might ask us. What is our response? It is like the parable where the landowner asks the same question and first man says, "Yes," but then never shows up and the second man who says, "No," changes his mind and works in the fields.

How hard is it to "yes" to the unknown? We all know the answer to that question. Never quite knowing what's behind life's corner is what our "yes" yields. (Is that what "blind faith" means?)

Our "yes" is based on a faith foundation that includes God's mercy, compassion and continuing presence. We may "blindly" say "yes" but our trusting eyes have the seen the glories of God and we are able to give our unconditional "yes" to life.

What does this life hold for us? Well, keep saying "yes" and then see what happens.

Catholics and the Journey

I asked an older adult who serves as a sacristan how the funeral went, since I was not involved. She replied, "Everyone who was Catholic, acted Catholic." At first I laughed it off but later thought what an unusual comment. And, a comment that only a Catholic would understand.

What she was conveying is that everybody who attended the funeral did what they were supposed to do, like receiving communion, standing and sitting at the proper times.

It occurred to me that Catholics are not very tolerant of those whose faith journey is different. We were taught not to seek clear answers to complicated and unanswerable questions. The Church (meaning hierarchy) did the homework for us. They thought through all the touch questions and our task was to absorb in three awful words that became a joke: "pray, pay and obey." If there was a Bible in a Catholic home it was meant for decoration, not digestion.

That kind of dim clarity provided our pathway to heaven. To take a moment or spend time questioning or reflecting on the beautiful mysteries of our Catholic faith suggests to others that this person may not be "Catholic." A "team player" we'd say today.

Like politics these days, questioning anything suggests unfaithfulness or disloyalty.

Is a Catholic response, "God forbid" we question God or is our response, "God bless" us who question and ponder those provided and assumed answers?

Hearing

Why do we clink wine glasses? To hear how much the glasses cost? No.

All the senses are experienced while drinking wine, except hearing. We **see** the wine color and some can tell the texture just from sight. We **touch** the glass as we raise it to the light. The wine's **aroma** is taken in. We taste the first sip which, again, the experts can quickly evaluate the wine's body. Then?

What no sound? I guess we could burp but that's crude. So what do we do complete our senses? We clink glasses to fill-out the sensual wine experience.

It's interesting because hearing is probably our weakest sense. Even in wine tasting it seems more as an add-on or to show friendship then something sensually essential.

The Church relies on hearing for so much of Scripture. How many times we've heard (there's that word again!) the words, "Hear the Word of God." The faith sequence begins with hearing and then moves to believing. And yet, hearing is the weakest. Tell a story to any friend and have him/her recount what you've said and you will uncover and hear a second, new story.

Not enough practice given to our ears? I guess. Our other senses are so busy absorbing information that hearing takes a second place.

We even remind ourselves to look at one's actions instead of the spoken word. And yet again, the spoken word is so crucial to Scripture.

Why not become more aware of our other senses and then combine them to our gift of hearing and from there, discern and experience what is being conveyed.

Life without hearing would be sad; never being able to completely savor the wine drinking experience. How incomplete.

"in-between time"

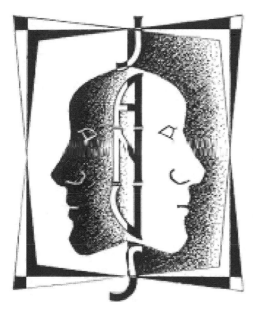

One of my favorites concepts is, "in-between time." It's not even a word but it is sure chock full of meaning for us. It's that space of empty time on either side of events.

Most of our lives is lived "in-between." In-between yesterday's event and the upcoming. Between Christmas and the New Year is truly an in-between space of empty time. I think that it's the most in-between of any week of the year. If you wish someone "Merry Christmas" during that week, well, it just sounds awkward. Unfortunately that greeting expires December 26. You are unable to say "Happy New Year" because people will think that you're jumping ahead of yourself unless you are planning on not seeing them again until the new year. In doubt, we resort to the tired and true, "Hi." Or, "Merry New Year?" Nah, it'll never catch on. We're stuck in the "in-between."

Some people hate life's "in-betweens". Divorced and remarried within a year. God forbid an in-between-time-breather to weigh your life. Going from one party to the next and you'll end up in rehab. Doing nothing creates an encroaching boredom. Without something, at least once in awhile, there would be no in-between time.

The Church says that our whole lives is one big "in-between" time. We were with God before birth and return to His care after our death. Suddenly our patience kicks in and we don't seem to mind life's waiting part so much.

And, how can you actually be "in-between" time when time continues to tick? Am I able to crawl between the first minute and the second and live "in-between" the two of them, at least for a while?

We can kill it, schedule it, race toward it, measure it, remember it, point toward it, generalize about it, count it, pass it, be on it, repeat it, share it, stretch and season it; stage, patch and trim it; we've had the best of them, the golden of them and the prime, peak and length of them.

And, we can be in it and enjoy the "in-between" of them as well.

Harvey Sinatra

"All right. So Frank never talked about me. Probably denied me everyday to himself, but, I'm real. I was a part of Frank's life from the beginning to the very end. It's amazing how much he listened to and followed my advice.

If things were going really well in Frank's life, I would be the voice inside him reminding him how weak he really was; how unsatisfactory and poor was a performance, a show or a conversation. I found that he would listen intently as I listed off all his deficiencies and weaknesses. I thought this was important for Frank to hear. I was the realistic in his life. I was his practical voice. All his wild dreams and imaginations needed to be trimmed and tailored. The voice of reason fell to me fell to my big and listening ears.

It was my responsibility to tell him to spend more money when a good impression was needed. It was me who told him to break off friendships which didn't produce anything good for his career.

Speeding up through a yellow light was my idea also. Walking faster and ahead of the old lady carrying groceries was mine. Getting angry and wildly throwing things was my way of alerting Frank to make himself known and that no one could push him around. It was only practical for Frank to think of himself first.

"What's in it for me?" was my daily mantra to him.
"Stay in bed a little longer"
"That's good enough, so just stop"
"No one will notice that you messed up, keep on going"
And there's always something ahead so "don't look back" were among my favorite remarks to him.

I even provided religious advice. That was the most fun for me. Teaching and reminding Frank about an angry and vengeful God kept him close to me. Constantly warning him that God's goodness and mercy was way too advanced for him kept him mine. An endless listing of his sins really endeared him to me. And, it is not only the listing, it is also the fact that there was nothing he could do about it that sealed our lifelong relationship.

You see, happiness is elusive and random. My buddy-buddy relationship with Frank was built on that elusiveness. How can anyone have what is elusive. That's the practical guidance I offered. It paid off. We had a solid and wonderful friendship his whole life.

I tried a rabbit character with another celebrity but it didn't work out. The practical, realistic, keeping-you-down rapport is the one that works best. Telling him that "It's okay to break a promise." That's me. "Take the easy way, life's hard enough." Guess made that up? "Everybody's got it better than you." Moi. Entering and leaving church feeling unworthy. A golden oldie from my mouth to his thoughts. "Why try. Is it really worth the effort?" Mine. "Looking out for 'number one' really looks out for everyone else!" Illogical but he always bought it. My idea. Why, I bet there's a

"Harvey" in your life as well. Living, breathing, influencing and holding you back and down every day."

"A Fish Story"

She enjoyed fishing with her family along Lake Michigan. She was the lucky one. Her spot caught all the perch. "Let me go where you are," laments a cousin. "O.k.," and she moves. No perch is caught by the new person in her spot. Is it luck? Is it a person's disposition? Or, is it both.

A "fish story," by the way, is a story that is rarely true. We've all heard them. Rich, colorful, long on detail but sadly exaggerated. Most real fishermen would not even consider perch to be fish, so perhaps this story is indeed not true.

Jesus caught fish. He even caught fisherman. Why fishermen? How should I know? Gullible? Susceptible to new talk about a kingdom that is of this world yet not of this world? Susceptible, meaning open to a shift in thinking? The word can be used in a positive way as well.

The first fisherman of Jesus became the first pope. Since then, we have been fishing for answers ever since. Fishing for the truth. Fishing for answers to age-old questions.

Often in our lives, we hook onto a belief in the hopes that it will carry us through all times of our lives. And it does, for a while. Then a new belief comes along and we find ourselves hooked once again. Hook-able people, I guess.

And then there's the one that got away. The regrets that life deals us whether we like it or not. Regrets that linger and hover unless they are tended to in one way or another.

I'm sure that you're thinking that the image of a fish is hardly a reflection but isn't fishing what life is all about?

In our patient waiting for something greater than ourselves to occur. We may say to ourselves, "I'm using the right bait but there's no pull. What am I not doing?"

The hooks that links someone you love for over sixty years of marriage. The hooks that bring children to love and care for into your life.
As we age, we learn to live with regrets - that's the fish that got away - things left unsaid, unforgiven, unknown consequences to a silly remark.

Jesus used fish to demonstrate the greatest act that we recreate every time that we gather in church. Five loaves and two of them. Only that small amount to feed a multitude. How on earth could he do that? How in heaven's name could he do that? Even his followers second guessed him, "Silly man, to think that he could feed a crowd this large with such a small portion. Two perch from Lake Michigan and five loaves from the local bakery. And is perch even considered a fish?

After the large crowd was fed, there were twelve baskets left over. Something complete happened during the feeding of the crowd. Jesus showed us perfection. The perfect number 7 and the perfect number 12. Perfect. Our efforts are never short of perfect. In failure or success, our efforts are perfect.

From among the smallest of creatures, the perch, we are full, sustaining, nurturing, loving and caring. Their is nothing fishy about our Christian faith. And if you're fishing for a clever conclusion, here it is. It's finding the right spot on Lake Michigan or a lake near you to fish for and hook yourself some perch.

"Churching" It Up

A friend of mine asked me if I'm "churching it up?" I didn't think that church could be used as a verb but I liked the idea. "Churching it up." I answered, "Yes."

We "church" it up with words like "amongst," "Thou," "art," and "whilst." The last one not so much but if we thought we could get God to listen better, we'd sure start throwing in "whilst" a lot more in our thoughts and prayers.

I guess we sound more serious when we use words like that. It means that we're not using our everyday language but including some special words that will more easily be lifted up to the God's heavenly ears.

We'll use rote prayers, beads, litanies, century-old prayers - anything to get the Big Guy's attention. Facing a particular direction at specific times of the day, mats, labyrinths, kneeling, jobbing, silence, humming; an endless list.

Scripture says that God hears our prayers before we even make them, in whatever form. Our speaking them is, I guess, a validation of what God already knows. He knows that we know that He knows. (Draw a diagram, if you need to.)

All prayer is giving glory and praise to God. Whether the Packers win, we bury poor, old St. Joseph in the front yard, or throw salt over our shoulders - all prayer is giving glory and praise to God.

So we humbly say, "Blessed is He amongst us who whilst we live and to whom we owe our lives and art worthy of His love. Amen."

A Semi-Monthly Treat

I arrive for the Sunday 8:00 a.m. twenty minutes before the Mass begins. The parking lot has one other car. It doesn't bother me.

I enter the over 150 year-old church, modernized now and the usher immediately greets me. I grunt, half awake. I've been coming here for over fifteen years. Always the second and fourth Sundays.

When I began, I asked the pastor if he needed help. I already had a 10:00 a.m. Mass at work and could only do one at 8:00 a.m. although I'm not a morning person. I only wanted two Sundays a month (didn't want to be taken for granted.) He agreed. New pastor arrived, same arrangement. Another new pastor arrived, same arrangement.

I enter the sacristy and get vested. The sacristan has already prepared everything for the Mass and the grade school servers are slowly arriving with tussled hair and still seem to be enjoying their sleep.

I enter the church proper and take a pew to hear the song before Mass. I've learned that the prelude is always moving and prepares everyone for the service. A parishioner accompanies Michael Kaminski, the liturgist and pastoral associate on either a violin or trumpet, or both. Always inspiring and subdued.

7:58 a.m. arrives and you would think that Noah's flood hit the pews. They all enter. (I think they're all sitting at home waiting for just the right time before leaving.) This is when the hugs and smiles begins. One couple embraces another couple. Children dart across aisles to greet another school chum. (I'm thinking to myself, "It's only been a week since they last saw each other!") Young couples with their children (all neatly dressed), middle aged couples who are glad their children have moved out, seniors and a splattering of single people. Many sit in the same places. On many Sundays, someone approaches me during my moment of solitude to tell me of a death in their family or mention someone we both know or a sermon that they enjoyed (Or didn't). I smile, a brief shoulder touch and wish them a good day.

The prelude ends. We line up in back for the procession song, always uplifting and moving. (I usually want to go home after their opening song.

"Why continue?" I think to myself. We've just did it!) My opening remarks are made. The first reading is completed and a parishioner sings a psalm that would put many popular singers to shame. (Again, I want to just go home because we have done it already *again*, but, alas I have to stay.) The second reading ends.

We all sit patiently waiting for me to stand for the "Alleluia" and the reading of the gospel. I wonder how long I should sit there before standing. It's so quiet now. So much has happened already and they still want more? Each time I think to myself before standing, "Do you have something to say today?" I, luckily answer "Yes." So I stand and the "Alleluia" begins.

After the gospel, it's my turn to turn those ancient readings into something contemporary. What can I give them to take home? It usually amounts to one word. I wish to leave them with one word to ponder or to consider. The sermon is never longer than five minutes. I get bored and I'm sure they do too. It's our fast-paced culture and my poor word power. I make them laugh but I hope I make them think. And, I wish that they might relive some of my thoughts during the new week.

They pay me to do this twice a month, not a lot but it's nice. Don't ever let them know that I'd do it for free. It's Church. It's families, born by blood and by faith. It's folks celebrating their lives as best they can. It's a twice a month treat for me.

"Let Go and Let God?" I Don't Think So

That phrase has been echoed often during my priesthood, especially with my work with the divorced and separated. It says to me that they want to have nothing more to do with this predicament, soooooo, "Let go and let God," It's just too difficult to handle by myself."

Oh, good. Now it's God's problem. Is this petition from you then filed away and on to the next issue? What does God now do with them? Wrath? Mercy? Slow or quick death for that unfaithful husband?

Passing off a problem, even if it's to an omnipotent and almighty Being does not dismiss our personal responsibility and involvement.

Trust in God. It has a magical sound to it. What will God now do with my trusting soul? What happens to my soul once entrusted to God.

Two things are occurring here. Free will and the God of my life.

Free Will is the role of being free to live our lives as best we can with the information that we have. Information. That horrible word which reminds us of the personal homework we haven't done yet. Giving it over or letting it become God's problem releases us from our homework. There is no magic pill, no magical prayer, there is no dismissal bell for the life we are living or haven't lived.

The God of My Life is looking in the mirror giving us a glimpse of who we think God is. Our image of God is often a projection of ourselves. (Original sin, anyone?) "I think that God is kinda of a hanging back sort of guy, easy going and quick witted. Oh, wait? That's me!" Limiting God, limits ourselves.

"Letting" God dismisses us. "Giving" or "Offering" to God our heartaches and pains brings those pains back to us. Sooooo, we're back where we started. Now what?

Ethel & John

Ethel died several June's ago after a full and rich life. Widowed at an early age, she returned to school earning her masters in journalism while teaching and raising two young boys. She worked her way through Catholic circles until becoming executive publisher of our weekly Milwaukee Catholic newspaper.

Her writing was always crisp, clean and clear. I'm sure she would use her red pen on my short reflection about her here. She wrote especially about social and injustice issues. The personalities surrounding them would inspire her allowing her articles to come to life for us, her readers.

Graceful in both her attire and hospitality, Ethel's house was full of angels. Not just any angel. Only the ones with a trumpet were allowed to adorn her home. The newspaper was called "The Catholic Herald" and she was a "herald of good news" (the paper's banner) both at work and in her personal life. The good news that she offered weekly was a hope-filled Church dedicated to addressing any issue that either held people back or denied them dignity or respect.

Her birthday was at the end of December. Later in her life, each year she would acknowledge a new friend with a small token of appreciation. I called it an "award," though she never laughed. She meant it as a sign of gratitude for another year of her life and the inclusion of someone new in her life.

She died on John the Baptist's birthday. Planned? Who knows. The first herald brought a message of preparation and renewal. The herald in my life brought a message of hope, joy and possibilities.

Both were Advent people everyday of their lives. Both lived remarkable lives. One may have eaten locusts but I'm sure that it was Ethel who suggested putting a little wild honey on it.

Finding the Holy Grail

The adventure and mystery surrounding the Holy Grail continues to this day. The cup of Jesus intrigues and captures our imagination. I hate to bust your fantastical thoughts but the Holy Grail has been found. (Tell Harrison Ford that he can go home.)

It is the hand of the teenager who he caresses and cleans his cell phone for third time in one minute.

It is felt by the warmth of your HDTV after a full evening's viewing

It is in the dogeared pages of a book you've enjoyed for years

It's in the silence of a sixty year marriage when a smile suffices

It's the reaching the bottom of all the papers on the desk that kept you working late at night

It's the distant musings that distract you from your unsatisfying hourly job

It's the quiet moments that seem to quiet anxious hearts

It's the purposefulness of keeping a promise

It's the satisfaction of keeping that promise

It's responding to a child's nightmare in the middle of your sublime sleep

It's the petting of healing cat after a tumor is removed

It's the diligence to rewrite your document to say it clearly

It's the spontaneous moment to talk to someone

It's the winter mountains that your traveled so far to see

It's in the weekend wait for the results of your medical tests

It's the phone call we all dread but answer anyway

It's the joy of your child's first recital

It's the vigil with a dying parent when you'd rather be anywhere else but you know that you are where you need to be

It's in the burnt Thanksgiving turkey no one cares because you are all together

It's in the loneliness but oneness to be the last living person of your family

The search for the Holy Grail is over. You found it. It was right before your eyes all the time. St. Matthew said it best from Jesus, "Where you treasure lies, there will your heart be."

"The Young Rascals" & God

How can I be sure
In a world that's constantly changin'?
How can I be sure
Where I stand with you?

Lord God, if I knew where to begin, I guess I'd be praying to You but where to begin? If life is a deck of cards then I've been cut and cut again and dealt rotten, losing hands for years now.

The consistency I've looked for has eluded me since I was young. What makes You so sure that You're the "something" that is missing in my life. You've been so torn apart over the centuries, what makes You so sure that my trust in You is worth it? And, if You're not sure, then how can I be sure? Why should I trust You? Self-Confidence?

Whenever I am away from you
I wanna die
'cause you know I wanna stay with you
How do I know?
Maybe you're trying to use me
Flying too high can confuse me
Touch me but don't take me down

How can you escape God? For how many years and days now I'm sure that I'm doing my own thing. I'm the one in charge. It's a no brainier. These illusions of a "God," I find it amusing especially, listening to people who sound so dependent and wound up in this invisible thing that seems to roam the world and the other-world as well. How quaint. "I Don't Care?"

Whenever I...
Whenever I am away from you
My alibi is tellin' people I don't care for you

Maybe I'm just hanging around
With my head up, upside down
It's a pity
I can't seem to find someone
Who's as pretty 'n' lovely as you

I'm a hit at parties when the topic of God comes up. I can refute any argument they throw at me. It doesn't take much thinking, I just listen to their imaginary tales and point by point take them apart. I even get listeners laughing at the ease I can dismiss and show the fools the believers that are. Certainty Amid Doubt?

How can I be sure
I really, really, really, wanna kno-o-ow
How's the weather?
Weather or not, we're together
Together we'll see it much better
I love you, I love you forever
You know where I can be found
How can I be sure
In a world that's constantly changing?
How can I be sure?
I'll be sure with you.

What works at parties doesn't always cut it when I'm alone. In the quiet of the night my mind can wander and my mind even wonders. "Weather or not," misspelled but powerful in its meaning. There is no season to discovering who God is for anyone, especially for me. I don't see God as that constant in this ever-changing world but yet I wonder and wander sometimes who He can be and who He is in my life.

Oh, what the heck, go ahead and deal the cards one more time.

Enjoy this 1967 musical treat
by "The Young Rascals"

The Splendor of the Royal Priesthood

Middle class beginnings is your origin. The parish priest and his behavior and manners appears to be the life for you. The seminary high school at 14 years old is yours for either four or six years and while there you perceive a life of privilege and comfort all done in the service of God's people. (You'd have to be a priest to understand that sentence.)

During those formative years you're told, spoken, unspoken or witnessed) that you are special and the priestly life will afford you opportunities and openings unknown to others. As a boy it is very alluring and nurturing replacing the mother you left behind and now replaced by your new Mom, the Church.

College (or fancily said "Scholastic Studies") begins and there's a knock on your shared bedroom door. It's a monsignor (whose title means nothing, by the way) and he tells you that Rome has summoned you to finish your studies in the Eternal City. You are also told that all of your studies will be taught in Italian but not to worry. (It's a small price to pay for princedom.)

Now granted you've encountered very few, if any, "real people" during this time. Perhaps a token soup kitchen as a photo-op for your hometown diocesan newspaper (picked up by no other news outlet) while your parents both smile and cry that the son they created has succeeded in replacing one mother for another.

You are ordained a priest by a notable bishop and you're on your way toward upward and lofty work. (As in calling priests on Monday mornings who didn't say the right words at consecration time and telling crying women that their annulment has been annulled, as in "you're out of luck but thanks for waiting for two years.")

Some of you may even study for a civil law degree which always amazed me in the Catholic Church in light of the priest abuse. (All those guys skipped the class on harming and sexually abusing children?) Many are now armed with degrees in canon and civil law and Church degrees that no one understands but has STD at the end of their names. (Most people don't wish to be associated with anyone with "STD" around their name!)

You surprisingly find yourself working in the Chancery Office (which separates you even further from "real people") and perhaps having a weekend Mass at a local parish where the pastor is already pastoring three parishes. You take one Mass and talk later to fellow priests about exhaustion from homily preparation and drive time.

After dutifully wearing french cuffs and the roman collar for years you finally receive the call from (yes) the Eternal City that you've been named a bishop but can't tell anyone for weeks until they do. ("Not even my mother, Mom?")

You are now in charge of a multi-multi million dollar complex that is complex with problems, crises and opportunities. You now wish that you spent a little more time in that soup kitchen.

For many years, that's been the Catholic bishop leadership. Or at least something close to it.

"Be Kind To Your KKKids"

"beep-biddly-oat-en-dodden-bo-bo-a-didden-dotten." That was the word my family created combining all the syllables I was unable to clearly say. (Can you sue your family for failed affection?) The other four siblings used this mocking word to tell me that I stuttered, as though I didn't already know it. My silent parents did not prohibit the word but their intervention might have proven helpful.

Stuttering among young boys is common, I'm told. "He'll grow out of it," say the experts. Sporadic stuttering throughout your life is another story, not mine. I know it's about to happen before I say the word. Usually in repetitive threes and in a staccato manner. Never four and rarely two, but three. (I think five is my record.) As in "ready, set, there's the word" I want to say but I can't say it. Whenever my threesome showed itself then the foursome quickly (and easily) sprouted out their created word to define me.

Called on in third grade by the gracious nun, I could not say my name. There was no threesome in those early years just a rapid succession of the beginning syllable. In third grade you're mocked, in the latter years the listening eyes just move downward as though they're saying to themselves, "Isn't there a drug this guy could take?"

Therapy was sought through the same order of nuns that politely afforded me more time than the other students to say a word or a phrase. This therapeutic nun calmly welcomed me to each session while my mother waited for me. I can still smell the starch of her religious habit and the antiseptic (non-smell) of her office space. She used a huge machine in those days, that would rival an MRI as it quickly flashed words in front me which I had to say

out loud. She often smiled at me as though she was saying, "You can come back next week but don't hold your stuttering breath." Sr. Francis Philip, God bless her. Kind and accepting to a youngster unable to say his name much less a complete sentence in public. She and I wrote a prayer to St. Joseph intended to have me identify with his quiet spirit. I regret to this day that I never saved her calligraphic prayer. She even used pseudo-parchment paper to show its holiness.

It's gotten easier in some ways. I've been in radio for over 25 years and preaching for over 37. The approaching word in my mind to be spoken still scares me. In a public forum or during a sermon, just try thinking of three synonyms for a word you'd like to say but not sure if you'll be able to. It's not so easy but it works for me.

I've come to accept it as I'm sure most people around me have. I'm as impatient as they are to hear the word that I wish to speak and that we both hear on its final third time around.

We live in an impatient world. We all know that by now. The word my family created for me was supposed to laugh me away from stuttering. It didn't work. But I'm able to laugh at myself. (By the way, my chuckles come in threes also.)

Creator & Creation Meet

(Frank Sinatra sings and St. Paul tells us the beautiful incarnation story.)

"She was Boston, I was Vegas,
She was crepe suzette, I was pie,
She was lectures, I was movies, but I loved her.
She was Mozart, I was Basie..."

God deemed angels not His equal but chose to take on human flesh.

"She was afternoon tea, I was saloon,
She was Junior League, I was Dodgers,
But I loved her morning, night and noon.
Opposites attract, the wise men claim,
Still I wish that we had been a little more the same..."

Emptying Himself of Divinity, He filled our Humanity with His Divinity.

"She was polo, I was race track,
She was museums, I was TV.
She did her best to change me
Though she never knew quite how,
But I loved her, almost as much as I do now..."

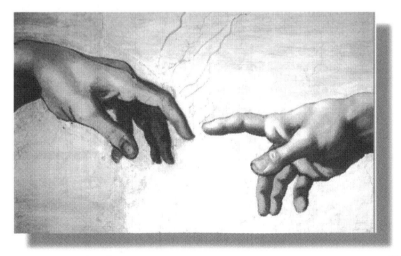

Jesus Christ being found in appearance as a man, He humbled Himself by becoming obedient to the point of death, even death on a cross. For this reason also, God highly exalted Him, and bestowed on Him the name which is above every name.

"She was Wall Street, I was pawn shop,
She was French champagne, I was beer,
She knew much more that I did
But there was one thing she didn't know,
That I loved her, because I never, never told her so..."

I heard a priest go to great pains to tell us about the separation between our Great and Almighty God and us, who are the lowliest of the lowly. I guess he missed St. Paul's Christological Hymn while in school. Too bad for him and his understanding of Christmas.

Sunday's Tuna

I suspect that it's the sound that triggers the gathering of my two cats into the kitchen on a Sunday night. We've done this for years now so I guess it's a ritual. No caregiver knows of this while I'm gone because it is my connection to my earthly felines who make the gift of their sleep enviable.

It begins with the simple grabbing of the can opener. How that one sound triggers in a purely instinctive brain and further triggers a reaction is beyond my analytical brain. (I've learned that I will never be able to eat a tuna sandwich in my humble home because of that one sound.)

I begin the circular opening and I need to not move my feet because two swinging tales now encircle me along with a whining chorus to a familiar weekly melody.

It's Sunday night. It's a simple treat. They devour it as only cats can - first with complete attention, an hour later semi attention and in the morning the clean bowls are ready again for the shelf; no washing necessary.

Is "yearn" too strong of a word? The Church doesn't use the word enough but St. Paul certainly does - we yearn for things and its satisfaction that are only found in Christ Jesus. The problem is not that we all yearn, we all do, but that we aren't always sure what our yearning is for or about? We think it's happiness when it may be chaos until we sort through and handle the chaos before attaining the happiness. It may be peace in spite of all the meetings and activities that we choose to consume our time.

"I want to be a better person than I am now," someone told me. "How do you do that?" as though I held a wise answer. St. Paul was so right. We "yearn" and he even goes so far as to use the word "groan." When was the last time you groaned?

Both life and religion is about expectation, wonder, anticipation, reconciliation and renewal. And it's also about those powerful words of yearning and groaning. If you don't know what you want then how can you ever achieve it?

One trigger tells my cats that it is again that time and the rest is instinct.

Pieces of Grace

"I'll have a host, a tiny sip of wine and several pieces of grace please."

You wonder during trying times but it arrives, just in the nick of time. Reflecting upon it later, you consider whether it might have been God's grace. What a great help to help us explain the good deeds done by us sometimes sinful people.

And it's not only a noun but a proper noun. It's also an adjective and even more it's a verb and an adverb. What a flexible word, this grace stuff. "Grace Kelly graced us with her effortless grace and graceful presence as she gracefully walked into the room." (Wow. There's grace all over the place. It's walking. No, it's on the table. No, it's over there.) It's rich in worth, effortless in its attempts and limitless in its quantity.

Alas, the Catholic Church needs to rein in this wild grace stuff and present it as a commodity. There are actually two form of grace, according to the one, true Church. Sanctifying and actual. Most Catholics can name those two graces, even on their deathbeds. What they may not know is that sanctifying grace is derived from the sacraments. When you participate in a sacrament you receive this elusive, rewarding, beautiful proper noun, noun and verb. Actual grace appears to appear when you need it the most. We cannot determine graces' travel time but we know that it's within us within nick's time.

It arrives just when you were about to say something questionable, zooming in from some unknown place. (I have yet to receive grace's reward during those occasions.) Another friend of yours dies and you discover a peace that baffles you. A serious discussion erodes and you feel you've said your peace and quietly listen. The same story is told to you for the third time and your newly found grace enables you to listen knowing there will be a fourth time. A serious diagnosis strips you of yourself but slowly and surely that noun/ verb creeps into every part of your being. A smile replaced a frown. The handshake is forgotten and a hug is provided. "If there's anything I can do for you," comes out of your mouth when there is nothing you can do.

Grace. It's a beautiful name. It's even a better as a verb when it travels by lightening speed to a noun within us. Our lives are graced. We can be grace to each other. Mary was full of it, so why can't we be? There is grace, in plentiful supply, thanks be to God.

"If Only..."

Well, here I am today in this time and place. Here I am. Right now. So why does my mind wonder and wander after hearing or thinking those two terrible letters? What can I possibly see in those two letters that could override or trump where or who I am today?

Two letters. It's not "Hi" which would mean that I met someone new today while being in this time and this place. "Hi" would mean an opportunity; a new door would be opened and connect me to this new person. Ahhh, alas, it seems that I prefer the other two-lettered word. Yes, you know it. I'll give you a hint, it has two letters. It's "if."

"If" has a life and a lifetime all its own. It can live and breathe almost with as much power and potency as the present chair in which I sit. Yet the mind is a hard thing to control as though it has a mind of its own. My mind can even add four more deadly letters with the additional word "only." Now I'm ready for a search less, worthless and futile backward journey that leads only to itself; in other words, it leads to nothing. "If only..."

"If only...?" Let's just dump the "only" part and concentrate on the two-lettered word that freezes and holds my breath - "if."

If only I took that job instead of the one I accepted then... (and now comes the three dots representing the unknown that reflects the unknown result of your un-chosen course.) See how this works?

It's a magnificent work of our evolved species. We humans have the unusual ability to look back and then choose a different direction or choice followed by romantically or foolishly filling in the unknown life that that unknown choice would have produced. (If you understood that sentence then you're as crazy as I am.)

"That other boyfriend. Yeah, the one you dismissed in favor of your husband. Yeah, he's best friend. Look how your life would have turned out had you chosen him?"

"If only your mom took that other street that she likes to get to work instead of the street she took when her car crashed into another one."

"In the '70's, if you invested in IBM you'd have that yacht that no one else on the block has."

We crazy humans even combine the missed past with a pretend future. "If I did X years ago I'd have Y now!" We have now completed our craziness by marrying a fake past with an artificial future.

The most convenient word we have at our disposal is comprised of only two letters. Convenient because we can't do anything about our situation. It's convenient because it's safe, there is no risk in reshaping a past, there is no investment in illusions. A mere two letters summarizes our perceived present lives. "If."

"If only Jesus didn't talk so much and did more." "If only he jumped down from the cross to show us who he really was!" "If only he listened to his mom and made the Cana wine earlier." "If only Jesus followed the rules to get what he wanted." "If Jesus only told us what he really meant instead of those silly, nonsensical; what did he call them 'stories,' no it wasn't stories it was 'parables.' I mean, what if?"

"If." Two haunting letters that haunt me each new day that I'm alive. Two letters that live in a imitation place within a flawed heart.

"Oh no! There was a social I wanted to attend this afternoon. I got all caught up in the "if" of my past that I missed it. Oh well, back to my 'ifying.'"

Enjoy David Gates singing his 1975 hit, "If"

An Angel & A Bird Converse

(First conversation, notice the subject of each sentence)

Angel: "I was made by God, you know the "Big Guy." My wings are bigger than yours.

Bird: "Dude, I can fly through all kinds of obstacles and never get thrown."

Angel: "I can talk to people on earth about important things that effect their lives."

Bird: "I can build a nest in nothing flat and create a brood of new Mes."

Angel: "I look human but I'm not which is what makes me marketable and a commodity for human consumption."

Bird: "My life is shorter, indeed, but my experiences are vast and enveloping."

Angel: "I can both think and have wings."

Bird: "I can fly. Enough said!"

(Another version of the same conversation)

Angel: "You're wings are smaller than mine but I noticed that you fly much faster and higher than I can."

Bird: "Yes, but yours are more appealing to the masses and the mere ornithologist only lists me among the others of my kind."

Angel: "But you are God's creature?"

Bird: "Yes, but you are a creation of God."

Angel: "Do you mean that I am a creation of God's imagination and not real?"

Bird: "Yes, you are invisibly real. Ummm, is that even possible?"

Angel: "I guess that it is. You can see from my picture that I'm ruminating with my hand to my chin. What's with that?"

Bird: "I think it means that I'm looking out for my next meal and you're looking out for all those people who look like you only without the wings."

Angel: "That's a scary thought. Do you think I make a difference in the world or just another ornament for their shelf?"

Bird: "Look. You have it all over Mary Martin. I can fly faster and higher than you on any given day but you can influence and effect (or is it affect, I always get those two mixed up.)

Angel: "You really think so?"

Bird: "Look again. Birds are for amusement without names or practical purpose but you guys influence, touch and invade human hearts with gentle and loving thoughts.

Angel: "Wow, I'm glad I'm an angel but what about you?"

Bird: "Don't worry about me. I see a worm over there so I'll humor the neighbor with my flurry, frantic flight.

The Right Person for the Right Job

Would you trust an optometrist who wears "coke bottle" glasses? Wouldn't you say to him, "Thanks for your time but no thanks?" Would you allow a dentist with brown, dirty teeth to examine yours? Wouldn't you say to him the same thing you said to the eye doctor?

Would you see a heart specialist who's smoking in his office with an ashtray full of butts? You'd say the same thing as you said to the eye-guy and the teeth-guy. Would you trust a heavyset priest? (I won't go there…) How about hiring a carpenter with soft, smooth hands or employ a construction worker with clean fingernails?

Professions need to fit your personality, demeanor, temperament; your passion. As much as I may wish to be an astronaut, it just ain't gonna happen.

Isn't that what the Christian faith is all about too? It's the right fit in the right person at the right time. It's not the smiling that makes a Christian a Christian. I'm starting to believe that the Christian faith finds you, not the opposite. For me, as for many, it's the "family religion." It suited my parents so why not me? And, like a good suit, it fits.

Anybody can smile. It's not the crying either. It is the meaning behind the action, it is the reason for that smile or those tears that makes the crucified Christ and the risen Christ the passion of our lives. Mirrors are never mentioned in the Bible because I guess they were invented yet. (1835,

Wikipedia says. But what about a puddle!?) That means all those Biblical characters never saw themselves except in a puddle. The best mirror of all is Christ because we finally got to see God. We say all the time that "nobody's ever seen God." How wrong if we have Christian eyes. I see God everyday in his creation and I don't mean only in nature. He lays His creation before us to see and behold because he visited here once.

Growing up under difficult circumstances make for an easy excuse the rest of your life. You can always blame the circumstances of your youth and then milk it for all that it's worth for the rest of your life. "Ahhh, that's the reason she acts the way she does."

Some people are suited for their job which makes them no longer jobs but professions, careers. Others tolerate their jobs until they can retire. My heart sinks when I hear someone boldly say that "it's just a job" as though it's a badge of courage worn by everyone. If it's luck or persistence, I've only had

comeuppance

What a weirdly spelled and spoken word for such a rewarding feeling. "He got what's coming to him," can be said and heard how often after reading the paper or watching the news. The trial dragged on, we learned names that we'll forget in a week, we formed an opinion before the trial began and like a sporting match we play it out until that weirdly spelled and spoken word is delivered.

I work with employees who can describe in detail, small details of nationally-played out trials as though it was the Packers versus the Bears. They'll never use that word but the meaning and feelings behind their words is crystal clear. "Revenge is sweet" is as weak a response as avenging is simply petty.

How many times in our personal lives do we wish someone we disagree with or dislike would just move away, find a new job, leave us alone or worse of all, die. "Comeuppance upon them," we think to ourselves. "Our world would be so be more enjoyable if only..." The first two words tell you the problem with that sentence. We should all carry a gavel around with us since we so often act as the arresting officer, the assistant DA, the jury and most importantly, the judge.

If you live long enough then you will get your comeuppance. Those you've doomed, will die; and now either the sweetness settles in or the unease of what your insignificant verdict produced within you.

It's another stab in our growing self-centered world where the "you" is the focus of everything and everyone. In our judicial expertise we have deemed that person and that other person other there to be gaveled for comeuppance. We patiently wait until our justice is rendered and redeemed. Yet what redemption is found in personal disagreements, lost marriages, misunderstood friendships, or a trial in which we actually do not know or met one of them?

But it feels good, this comeuppance stuff. And feeling good is what matters, isn't it?

Friday Nights, 1965

Every Friday night after school my sister and I had to walk to the Conservatory of Music for our piano lessons. It was the last thing we wanted to do but the choice was not ours. We'd walk the twenty minute Manitowoc walk. The nun who taught me probably escaped the Nuremberg trials and was now available to teach frightened young children the instrument of their choice. I was never that good on the piano but its appreciation of music is still with me today.

When my sister couldn't join me, I would make the walk alone to my grandmother's house, a short block away from the Conservatory. There, she would make me a braunschweiger with onions sandwich (healthy eating was not a big deal in those days) and my Friday Evening Television Ritual would commence .

CBS, 6:30 "The Wild, Wild West" - James Bond on a horse.
7:30 "Hogans Heroes" - a WWII prisoner of war camp which my nun piano teacher could well have run.
8:00 "Gomer Pyle, USMC" - silly but endearing.
8:30 Break time. I didn't like "Mr. Roberts," so it was a good time to stretch.
Switch to NBC, 9:00 "The Man from U.N.C.L.E." - James Bond in the future.

A complete evening of music appreciation, high fat pork and a heavy dose of "color" television (which our family didn't have).

My walk home was always satisfying and full of contentment. And, it probably burned off some of that liver sausage as well.

A Spatula for Jesus

It was kept in her kitchen drawer so I could easily grab my wooden prop when visiting my grandmother on the many days my mother would say to me, "Go do something!"

She'd begin her nap and hoping not to be nabbed, my pretend quiz show would begin in her back bedroom. I wonder now if she wondered while falling to sleep if psychiatric help was available for me in our small town.

This was my time facing her two empty walls but seeing my imaginary audience. Holding the spatula firmly in my 11 year-old hand I was all those men I tried to imitate – Don Pardo, Jack Kennedy, Gene Rayburn, Johnny Olsen, and how many others a young mind absorbs. It was my glorious sixty minutes while snoring was faintly heard down the hall and a promised braunschweiger sandwich when she awoke.

My stuttering stopped, my poise increased, my delivery was clear and clever as I delivered a message of hope and joy in front of a congregation surrounded by stained glass windows where my grandmother's one window once was. I think she's still napping down the hall while I'm still holding a wooden spatula provided to me by my grandmother.

Often after Mass I still wait for her braunschweiger sandwich. Back then it was pretending to be all those people in my grandmother's back room and now it's providential pretending to be who I'm called to be in front of you.

Salvation & My Toilet

The toilet had a "thing" that wasn't working. (I didn't know the technical name.) It was in the back part, whatever that's called. Being a college graduate I was confident that I could and should fix it.

After numerous attempts, I destroyed the thingamajig and no longer had a working toilet. It's Sunday. (I have honored the third commandment). I give in and call a 24-hour service that offers "complete service." I now need to wait. And, wait and wait.

He finally arrives on this late Sunday afternoon and, after two minutes, fixes my "thing" (he had a name for it and I trust that he was correct) for $110.00. "Cash only." I gladly pay him and he departs for the next college graduate's toilet.

Religion Part

Salvation need not wait for death. Salvation is responding to a need that needs to be well, needed right now. The sin part is clear, I tried to do something for which I have neither the expertise nor the interest in completing (but need to us it). I committed a sin, of sorts.

Redemption is necessary in order for me to get on with my life. In no other words, I need a toilet!

The waiting is the worst part. Not the strongest of American attributes, but I waited and soon discovered that my bladder was working. I need a savior or I have no toilet. Is it ironic that it happened on a Sunday? Be that as it may, the savior (plumber guy) arrived...finally. He was a bit too chatty at the end when I needed to use my new, or now repaired, toilet.

A Happy Ending

The only part of my sad tale is the price. Our salvation was paid for in full by the sacrifice of Jesus Christ; my salvation on that Sunday cost a lot less but still a tidy sum.

On a late Sunday afternoon, I felt the sin, regret, anticipation, unworthy and then the redemption. Yes I experienced and felt true salvation.

Obsessed with "Three"

One or two? No, It's Always three.

What is it about the number three? Is counting to four just too much to ask of us busy and hurried people? Or is it that we just love the simple and what appears to be a complete number. Where would Christian churches be without the Trinity or "faith, hope and charity"?

Forget the four directions and four seasons, we are quite content with the lower number. (Actually, Wisconsin really has only three seasons, so the meaning remains strong!) But never four.

"Ready, Set, Go"
Green, Yellow and Red
third solider on the lighted match is shot
young, middle age and senior
Jesus, Mary and Joseph
low, medium and high
Larry, Curley and Moe
Patty, Maxine and Laverne
"A priest, a minister and a rabbi walk into a bar..."
three little words
"third time is a charm"
"three strikes and you're..."

small, medium and large
"coffee, tea or milk?"
yesterday, today and tomorrow

And, if you still don't believe me, just try making a four minute egg!

Four Wise Men?
"Three's Company"
"I will destroy this temple and in _____ days…"
In the tomb for how many days?
In the fish for how many days?
Mary visits Elizabeth for three months
Guests are like fish after…

The perfect number? I guess it fits our thinking patterns to think stuff in threes. Two doesn't offer enough of a choice and four is just, well, it's an extra thing to consider. Three just fits. Oskar Schindler's personal list of three was a good doctor, a forgiving priest and a good accountant.

Carl Jung, the psychologist, suggested that the number four is really the more perfect number. I don't think most people would agree with him. Which is the more perfect shape, the square or the triangle? Could the Christian church handle one more person in our heavenly observation deck? The Catholic Church is slowly suggesting that Mary, the mother of God, may one day join that group. But who knows.

After all, it would no longer be three.

It Takes Two

There's something about combining 1 and 1. Three Dog Night told us over forty years ago that "One is the loneliest number that you'll every do." You are only "terrible" for one year when your teeth are growing otherwise it is the combination of ones we cannot resist.

No, this isn't about marriage and that one and one are madly in love. Two marriages is common these days with even three creeping in as in, "ready, set, go." The "go" part seems to be the final one although I got to know and like both one and two.

"One" just doesn't seem enough. "Let's have one for the road," doesn't mean one but means the one added to the previous number. I have two cats. Seems right just in case one, you know, experiences that ninth live. For vacation I pack at least two of almost everything in case one proves to be not enough. I began to watch the movie "Noah" but stopped when hoards of animals are let on the ark when only two were permitted. (The only Biblical part of that film was its title.)

I keep a "second" cloak in my car in case someone asks me for my cloak as Jesus demands of me, "Sure, here you go" as I walk back to my car. Insincere or wise planning?

We have two arms and legs which suits us well in life's travels. You cannot have a war with yourself, even the Civil War was clearly divided into twos. Forget the distractions of sports when the two teams match and you're holding your second cup of beer with your second wife, your two children (one hers, the other yours), remembering that second mortgage on your home which explains the second job you have and your in-laws (two) visiting for the weekend (two).

There's two sides to most stories which we all refuse to believe in our rigid, single-minded views (Three Dog Night anyone?) We should all have two friends when one takes a second look at us. (Women seem to be much better at increasing friend size than guys are.)

All of our simplified-making life is based on that magic number: sin/grace, heaven/hell, God/devil, plaid/solid, up/down, inside/out and you already know, Democrat and we don't wish the second party on anyone, Ecclesiastes' solemn list of times all done in twos that most funerals seem to include and I've heard more than twice.

Stephen Sondheim gets his two cents worth with "Into The Woods" and the song, "It Takes Two,"

"I thought one was enough, It's not true: It take two of us You came through When the journey was rough. It took you. It took two of us."

Your crisis needs to be shared and you call your first friend who isn't home. You instantly call your second friend who answers never telling her that it's your second call. The second friend listens and you smile at the caring advice.

Before this gets to be too (couldn't resist) much, I end my tribute to twos. On second thought, I need to add for a second time the importance of twos in our lives. I found a sale online and bought two shirts. They arrive in... guess? Two weeks.

Micah 6:8

I was doing yard work today and saw a glint of a piece of paper near the garage. "More garbage from the neighbors," was my first thought. I reached down to pull it out and out came a strange, old map. I hurried upstairs to examine this unknown find. "Was it from previous neighbors?" "Are Indians buried here?" were among my thoughts.

I wasn't sure but I knew that I held in my hand what no one else had. I had found it. Do I tell anyone? Of course not. I'd have to share the rewards with them. "What rewards?" I responded to myself. (This occurs often when one lives alone, by the way.) "Why, the rewards that this map will reveal to me. It is so old, it must contain the secret to something mysterious that is unknown to everyone, except now to me.

Carefully, I unwrapped this found treasure (notice that now it's no longer just a "piece of paper") and carefully put on my reading glasses (age) and saw before me its colorful inscriptions and instructions. I was numb and speechless (a rare treat). Listed before me were three statements, all in English. (So much for the mystery of a foreign language to make this reflection more exciting.) The parchment (certainly no longer paper) read "to act justly, to love mercy and to walk humbly with God."
Micah 6:8

The contents were too much for me to digest in one sitting. I needed to put it aside for a while (three minutes) and then, possibly return and look at it once more. It was truly more than I could bear. "What does it mean?" I said to myself, alone in my home. "Act, love and walk" were the verbs. The nouns were clearly before me, "justice, mercy, God."

What did I fail to see all those years? Why did I flounder when the simplicity of it all was right here before me in threes. (Damn "threes!") I had found it. No, I had uncovered it. No, it was revealed for only me to see. I think thought that this was not mine, but ours. Not words to be share, but to become. Not hoarded by me but to be lived for the benefit of others. Not to be saved but to spent completely.

I, I mean we have found my, I mean our treasure.

Who's Petula Clark?

Getting Old Is Pretty Cool

I mentioned the song, "Downtown" by Petula Clark and my 40 year old co-worker asked me who she was. I was floored with disbelief. I didn't know where to begin.

If she didn't know about Petula, there was no point in talking about Bobby Vinton or Jonathon King. And, I could forget about mentioning Rosemary Clooney, a favorite singer of mine. (Isn't she the aunt of someone famous?)

It was among one of the signs that I'm now a part of a group whose membership I never sought.

I'm getting older. There are multitudes of people roaming around in my head that over half the population never heard of. Efrem Zimbalist, Jr. (Only really, really old people would know who the Senior was), David

McCallum, Eve Arden, Shirley Booth, Jack Kelly; just to name a few. Do I need to find a good nursing home to reminisce about the names I grew up with? Do I need to surf the web more to learn the occupations and names of people in their 20's? Am I resigned to TV Land television for the rest of my life (which is getting shorter each year, by the way). Do I become one of those people who needs to convince young people that Petula Clark is worth knowing, only to have them humor me with their attention?

Musical Memories

These youngsters will never know the sweet sound of a scratchy 45-record played too many times on a Sears Silvertone turntable or the remedy for a warped album. Many Ray Coniff and Percy Faith albums were saved in our home.* But wait! Who knows who those people are or were anyway?

Aging Benefits?

Aging definitely has its benefits. You begin to speak more freely, not caring about the consequences. You find yourself willing to listen more, even to stories that you've heard before. Someone mentions something that happened forty years and it feels like yesterday to you. Now I'm able to order off the "senior menu" in many restaurants.

Oh well. It's now time to listen to the "The Guess Who" sing, "No Time." A timeless favorite.

Just In Case You Didn't Know

Efrem Zimbalist, Jr. - "The FBI"
David McCallum - "The Man from U.N.C.L.E."
Eve Arden - "Our Miss Brooks"
Shirley Booth - "Hazel"
Jack Kelly - "Maverick"

* You place the warped album under a throw rug and walk over it for two weeks. It bends back, truly.

The Unsung God

Playing Favorites

To play favorites is always a dangerous game. For a parent, it becomes quickly apparent which child is treated just a little better than the others. For an employer, it can be deadly if you hope to promote teamwork. (I often told my parents that I was the favorite of the five but they just continued to prepare supper.)

Playing favorites is risky business. To play this game with the deity can be especially so. However, at the risk of risking, I'll risk a little. God the Father is the Big Cheese, I get it. God's Son is at the right hand of God and all authority is granted to them. My favorite, though, is this Holy Spirit guy. Or is it a gal?

All the descriptions attached to the Holy Spirit have failed through the centuries. The Holy Spirit remains fluid, evasive, graceful, elegant, permeating and penetrating but always present.

Potency & Power of the Holy Spirit

Think of Tinkerbell on Ritalin and you get a sneaky idea of the powerful, potency and enveloping presence of this third person of the Trinity. And who's to say that there's a chronology to the Trinity? Why can't the Holy Spirit be first by breathing vitality into all creatures at the very beginning. The Holy Spirit is at the baptism of Jesus when the Spirit's announcement wasn't to be until Pentecost. I told you, this sneaky, pesky third-wrung of the deity.

I guess part of the reason I like the Holy Spirit the most is that you truly cannot capture the image of this person. The dove was a nice attempt but still too limiting for the force that the Spirit plays in our lives. Would wind be a better figure - try catching and holding "wind?"

Just when you thought that your life was breaking a part, something greater fills you up and carries you forward.
Just when you thought your child was lost to that city or that other religion, something bigger leads that child back to sanity.
Just when you thought that "so and so" would never give you the time of day, she tells you what time it is and then asks how you're doing.
Just when you thought you had life figured out, boxed up and wrapped tightly, a special delivery arrives with a new box that surprises you.

Just when you thought... feel free here to add your own "Unsung" interventions or intrusions or inspirations or interruptions or invitations or inclusions or reclusions or remembering or remorsing (new word) or reinventing.

I guess that's why I like the Holy Spirit more than the others. (Sorry, guys!) Just when I think something, the Holy Spirit fills me up with something more or something less.

God's Apology

Noah & The Flood

Have you seen those two words together? I bet we've thought about it often but never really thought that the Almighty would do it. God apologizing? Is it because of all the weird animals and rodents that He created? No. It was on our behalf. And God offers no apology for His apology. Public people always preface their apology with "If I have offended" as though an apology is not necessary but for those who need one, here's my "If-apology." That's not an apology.

Two Simple Words

We all know that an apology is two simple words. Even if the intention is not sincere, we are still moved to hear them after an injustice or harm is done to us. We may not even believe it but those two words continue to live in our hearts as we heal.

God apologizes to us for the flood. I hadn't considered the import of that story before but it is both unique and profound. **Unique**: one of a kind. I don't think God's apologized since. **Profound**: Well, it's God apologizing! He completely destroys the earth leaving us with an aging Noah, his family and two of all those animals we love and two of all the animals we hate. God then asks us to accept His apology. Even God doesn't turn back time's hands (If He can't do it then who can?). He lets the disaster stand. He allows the destruction to occur and hopes now to move on. The past is past. It cannot be undone.

Blame First, Then Think

"You misunderstood me," is what we would say to a good friend whom we've harmed. "It's not what you think that it is," is another popular phrase. Notice that both statements bring the attention back to the person harmed and not the allegedly harmer.

The buck stops with God. A buck that stops with a promise from God; no it's a commitment.

Through the centuries I think that faiths have weighed-in far too heavily on sin. I suspect It is a natural technique for a large institution to ensure survival - perpetuate something that makes people feel lowly to keep them coming back; and contributing. I fear that attending a church service because of a sin we've committed leaves us only with that sinful feeling when the service is complete. (Someone told me that sin is "self inflected nonsense.") Sometimes, I wonder about its truth.

Can we proceed one step farther and suggest that God needs to apologize because He committed a sin? (Where's the faggot and some steak sauce? "Suggesting" isn't heresy, it's just a consideration.)

Mutual Salvation

Humanity is in need of salvation by a merciful and forgiving God. That is 101 theology for any faith. It's a given for all of us who believe in something greater than ourselves.

In addition to Jesus Christ, is it possible that God is drawn one step closer to our lives because of the awful-flood-thing. God lets us know that great and small mistakes do happen but that "nothing left" does mean the end of the world.
(Sorry "Rapture folks.")

God apologizes and to show his sincerity He gives us a new covenant, a permanent sign of His apology. A rainbow. As Kermit sings, "The lovers, the dreamers and me." All three words add up to God. All three add up to the divine life that we all able to live each day - full of grace and full of sincere apologizes.

Our Backpacks

Another Labor Day passes, the grill is soon put away and the freshly laundered school clothes will be laid out for school children. That's right, it's now time to find your No. 2 pencil, backpack and return to school. No Bic pens for us back then, just a fountain pen (with ink all over our fingers) and our trusty and true No. 2 pencils.

I know. Many of you had to walk twelve miles, each way, to get to your school. Good for you. My school was only four blocks. It was a cinch.

But wait! A backpack? What's a backpack, we never had any of those.

Life's Backpack

The few school items we carried back then hardly called for what looks like a parachute for kids. No one had a backpack back then. Only soldiers carry backpacks, not kids.

As the years go on, however, we begin to create our own backpacks. They are full of memories, experiences and events. Some are them wonderfully happy, others begin to weigh more but we continue to carry them.

It seems, as the year progress, that our books and papers carried behind us gets heavier. A tragedy years ago, a misunderstood conversation that ended an important friendship, a hurtful divorce, or personal issues that continue to haunt and plague us.

No wonder adults have back problems!

We carry life's backpack where ever we go. We'd like to lighten its weight but it just seems to increase rather then diminish. No wonder adults have back problems! Carrying all that stuff all the time gets to be bothersome.

Jesus asks us to carry his weight on our shoulders. (Oh wait! I thought Jesus takes **our** burdens on **his** shoulders but not the opposite. This is weird.)

Jesus asks us to carry **his** weight of the world on **our** shoulders. Wouldn't that make our load even worse then it already is? Actually it doesn't. To carry our own, personal weight only bears us down personally and can often isolate us. Carrying the weight of others opens us up to the prayerful world of the concerns of and for others. It lightens our load, as Jesus tells us. "Take my yoke," he says.

So in our school year of life, let's lighten up a bit. Carry the concerns and loves of Jesus on our backs instead of the endless and unresolved weight of our past. We may find it both rewarding and even educational.

Catholic-Speak

Every discipline has its own language, sometimes shorthand, other times just to be verbose. It's the nature of the beast. If there was not a unique language or way of speaking, then everyone would want to join.

A Catholic Sample

Catholics are not exempt from their dazzling and baffling lingo that's fun at cocktail parties but does little to further God's kingdom in this world or the next.

Take for example

Hypostatic union = three persons in One God. (Why not just say that!)
Hermeneutics = interpretation (or is it your bartender's name
"Mysterium tremendum et fascinans" = "wholly wow!"
Catechetical = teaching
Sitz im Leben = "Just tell me what's going on, right now"
Apologetics = "Explain something that can't be explained, please?"
Discernment = "Just think about it before acting foolishly"
Sacramentary = the big book the priest holds or the young altar server
                who can barely lift it
Alb = a male dress, usually white, that helps you stand out in a crowd
Sacorium = a Catholic sink
Exegesis = "Where are you right now?"
Crozier = a Bishop's cane, regardless of his age
Cinture = a priestly belt, you don't want to know what it stands for, not pretty
Purificator = a Catholic towel
Presider = Me (formerly Officiant, then a Celebrant, then a President)
Purgatory = a rest stop before the big stop
Limbo = no where to put you for centuries but now happily forgotten
Legion of Decency = stops you from seeing the good movies
Intinction = dip the wafer in the wine (frowned on)
Monstrance = a fancy, way-over-priced wafer holder

Ready for the test?

I hope you're not laughing because I had to learn all that stuff.

Wrestling with Prayer

Pinned by an Angel

Jacob wrestles with an angel in the Book of Genesis. He loses, as though he thought he could pin a messenger of God.

Prayer is a wrestle. Even the sound of the word, wrestling, has a struggling sound to it. Americans have it pretty easy and we can't figure out why praying to God can't be easy too. We love to control things and, as life goes on, finally figure out that there is very little that we can or do control.

Jacob is attempting to find his place in the world. Is he the leader of his people or it is someone else? What should he do with his life? Who should Jacob trust in discerning what will happen to him? He wrestles with an angel throughout the night. Coincidence that it's during the night? Not quite. What better time for life to invade you than in the darkness of your life. The angel changes Jacob's name and injures him. He thigh is wrenched (another great word).

Prayer is a Commotion

Jacob becomes the leader of his people and fathers the Jewish people that we know today. All done through the high school sport and fake sport that so many love to watch.

Prayer is a commotion that breaks into our lives. If we initiate prayer then we pretty well know the direction it's going to take. We know how it's going to end. We ask for something, God doesn't give it, so we stop praying. Sound like a true American?

Catholics pride themselves on their "pat" prayers. Just say this paragraph or repeating this sentence fifty times and you've done your part - that's Catholic prayer. Rote and repeated. An older priest told me that he no longer can pray. (Only Catholics can understand that sentence.) What he's saying is that he's no longer to say the Mass prayers or or set prayers of the Church. I wanted to tell him that now he is able to finally "wrestle with prayer" only without the Catholic ropes tying him down. (I chose not to say that because of his age.) Without the repetition he could be able to finally discover the commotion which is natural to prayer. Am I doing all the talking or does shutting a bit help in this earthly-divine exchange?

Prayer is commotion where God breaks into our lives and influences us. God doesn't tell us what to do or how to do it. God influences and inspires. (How else would you want a Creator to act?)

"Face to Face"

Prayer is a struggle that is intended to be messy, unclear and confusing. God's prayer is an intrusion into our comfortable lives inviting us to a deeper appreciation of life or asking us to limp a little more. If the leader of the Jewish people limps knowing the cause is from God, can we ask anything less of ourselves when face to face with our Creator? That's what Jacob names the angel who wrestles with him, "face to face with God."

Perhaps that's the best definition of prayer.

Prioritizing Through Prayer

Decisions, Decisions

Years ago folks in Wisconsin had a big decision to make. Which television program do they watch? The Milwaukee Brewers were doing very well, the Green Bay Packers had their first game and the president of the United States was set to address Congress on the jobs problem.

I did not see a big decision to be made and knowing Wisconsin folks I know what their preferences were. I chose the political choice. Not being home at that time, I set the recorder.

Keeping the Focus

Prayer is a prioritizing experience. It is a, as often as you think necessary, method to keep your focus clear. As the country/western song sings, "Who's Your Daddy?" What is the source of your energy and passion? Recognizing that can only strengthen whatever resolves you've made for yourself. Taking it a step further, could not those resolves be not just your work but the collective efforts of you and your Creator?

Prayer is that unique opportunity that brings you back to the life's basics. There's no kidding around, you don't need to pretend or exhibit pretense. You simply let yourself go and let yourself fall back into those trusting, strong arms.

Prayer & Petitions

Those who attend Sunday church services must get sick of praying for peace only to read the Monday newspaper. How many years can we continue to hold out that virtue until it becomes real?

The 9/11 anniversary was here again and I read two wonderful articles. The first praised the U.S. aggressive acts of the past years assuring readers that it was worth it and that we are truly safer because of them. The second article used the Norway terrorist act of that time as a comparison to our 9/11. The prime minister quoted a young girl who said, "If one person can cause all this terror, how can a hundred of us show love, peace, community and harmony."

Is our prayer of peace to God each week asking God to do something for us or to inspire us to work with Him in our lives, in our relationships, in our attitudes. Prayer helps keep our priorities in a proper order.

I missed the president's address. The local station listed his address as scheduled but played the Packer game instead. Welcome to Wisconsin's priorities!

"If one person can cause all this terror, how can a hundred of us show love, peace, community and harmony."

"Send In The Clowns"

Isn't It Rich?

Isn't it rich?
Are we a pair?
Me here at last on the ground,
You in mid-air.
Send in the clowns.

God and me. Who would have thought it could happen. Why, I think it's a relationship made in heaven. I shouldn't be surprised though. Why would a creator not care for the His creature. Like a good movie, you want to see how it ends. (Even if you've seen the movie before.) Too bad we keep missing each other. He's way up there somewhere and I'm stuck roaming around down here.

I think of St. Paul and his beautiful prayer that says Jesus didn't deem equality with God something to be grasped at but, instead, emptied himself taking on our life.

Wow. I keep looking up toward heaven while Jesus is here within and through me everyday. (No wonder my neck always hurts!)

A Little History on "A Little Night Music"

Stephen Sondheim writes in his book, "Finishing the Hat," that the song was originally intended for a male but the writers thought that a woman should sing it since she did not have that many songs in the show, "A Little Night Music," 1973 with 601 performances.

He'd written songs before for specific singers like Ethel Merman's "Everything's Coming Up Roses" in "Gypsy;" Elaine Stritch's "The Ladies Who Lunch" in "Follies;" and now for Glynis John it was to be a simple song called "Send in the Clowns."

Isn't It Bliss?

Isn't it bliss?
Don't you approve?
One who keeps tearing around,
One who can't move.
Where are the clowns?
Send in the clowns.

I wake up the morning all set to go and retire to bed at night wondering what I've done. The gift of life that God's given me is bliss. Perfect and great, happiness and joy. Before my head hits the pillow, can I not smile softly knowing that His approval is enough for my worth? There is no need for searching the clowns, they do not need to be cued in - they are right within me.

Just When I'd Stopped Opening Doors

Just when I'd stopped opening doors,
Finally knowing the one that I wanted was yours,
Making my entrance again with my usual flair
Sure of my lines,
No one is there.

I have arrived. (I'm a late bloomer!) My confidence, self-esteem and worthiness are all in tact. In fact, I feel very competent and most capable. I often felt that this humility thing in churches is overrated. Can't one be both competent and humble? At the same time? My neck already hurt from always looking up; now it has to hurt because my head is hanging low! I'm sure of what I know. Because now I know that I don't know.

Why Such A Hit? The Writer Has No Clue.

"Why so many fine (and not so fine) singers have recorded "Send in the Clowns" is a mystery to me," Sondheim writes. "I don't think the song is eminently worth singing, but why this balled of all the ones I've written?"

"Then Judy Collins recorded it in England, where it incomprehensibly became a hit, after which Frank Sinatra's recording made it an even bigger one, and soon enough virtually everybody in the pop field climbed on the bandwagon."

Don't You Love Farce?

Don't you love farce?
My fault I fear.
I thought that you'd want what I want.
Sorry, my dear.
But where are the clowns?
Quick, send in the clowns.
Don't bother, they're here.

Thinking the opposite or contrasting my views against others has been my MO for a long time. Never taking myself too seriously has allowed me to stand up and speak in a large crowd. A moment of doubt becomes the traction I need to propel myself to the next project or event. Remembering the 8th grader who pretended to say Mass enables me to preside over the Eucharist. St. Paul calls Christians "fools for Christ." Not quite the lofty title you'd give to priests, bishops or the pope. "You fool," suddenly becomes a compliment.

It is foolish to forgive when you're angry and it is folly to smile when you're a big frown. I don't need to look for clowns, I have a mirror in my bathroom.

Only Barbra Streisand Could Pull This Off!

According to Sondheim, Barbra Streisand wanted to record the song but some lyrics did not make sense to her. He said that she felt there was an "emotional gap, so when she asked me to write something that would accomplish the transition, it seemed a logical request rather than the whim of a diva."

So instead of the stanza beginning with "Isn't it rich," Sondheim wrote this for Barbra:

"What a surprise! Who could foresee I'd come to feel about you What you felt about me? Why only now when I see That you've drifted away? What a surprise...What a cliche..."

Isn't It Rich?

Isn't it rich?
Isn't it queer,
Losing my timing this late
In my career?
And where are the clowns?
There ought to be clowns.
Well, maybe next year.

We end with the opening question. Rich. The wealth of God's love against my poverty standing next to Him. The huge bank balance that was He's Son sacrifice becomes my down payment for joy. During the Mass, the beautiful phrase is said, "as we wait in joyful hope..." Waiting generally generates impatience unless that waiting is done in a "joyful hope." Two powerful virtues weigh in to my waiting. Now it's both waiting and arrival. Where are the clowns? (I thought I told you.) It's us. God's beautiful creation of clowns dancing together in the circus of life. Rich indeed, we are.

Enjoy the original singer of "Send In The Clowns," Glynis John

Life's Six Nouns

"I've been a puppet, a pauper, a pirate, a poet, a pawn and king," sang the guy who knew what each word meant in his own life.

If you think about your life as a musical composition you might appreciate what Sinatra's singing about. A symphony is comprised of movements that savors where you are presently or moves you on to life's next movement.

We can luxuriate being "king" but that title definitely has a "shelf life." As of this writing, Queen Elizabeth II is the longest reigning leader in the world (with little power or authority but still lots of pomp) right behind Fidel Castro who passed away. (Both of them governed islands. Coincidence?!)

The magic of life in all its musical notes teaches and reinforces; teaches again and then reinforces once more – complete with sharp and flat notes that either others intone upon us or they become the notes playing loudly in our heads. ("Growing Pains," anyone?)

Don't worry about me taking each of those nouns apart and boring you with a list. But how about those times (As in, all the time?) when all these "Sinatra Nouns" play in our head.

"Puppet, Pauper, Pirate, Poet, Pawn, King." (Should have chosen "Prince" for the last noun – for symmetry's sake, oh well.)

You're at work and I'm at the altar at Mass and we enact a daily symphony of six movements in one resounding, unrepeatable performance.

Puppet, for the corporation we represent; **Pauper** for the paycheck we never think is enough; **Pirate** for retelling stories others told us and making them our own; **Poet,** we do have moments when the words spoken are truly ours; **Pawn,** who else can do our job either better or more cheaply and **King,** we're the one doing it right now, this very moment and we love it.

All six nouns are accomplished in one or two sentences, said to a fellow employee on a typical morning and you walk away singing Frank's next verse…

"I've been up and down and over and out
And I know one thing
Each time I find myself layin' flat on my face

I just pick myself up and get back in the race..

 View a unique presentation of Frank's song, "That's Life."

Snow & Cancer

Around 5:00 p.m. the soft, fluffy white stuff slowly begins falling and a ballet can be heard in the background as the whiteness waves and winds itself to the earth joining other like-minded whitenesses – all done against an early evening's dark grey.

She told the doctor that she found a small lump and she told the doctor that she feels great but the tests show otherwise. Both admit that something can happen with this fragile life – at any age.

He calls his wife to the window and says, "Honey, isn't this beautiful? What a great way to begin the Christmas season." She smiles back and says, "Yes, it's that special time of the year." (Ballet music continues in the background.)

"We can run tests to see what's going on," the doctor says to her while a doctor in the next room tells him that "This is common for men your age, you feel fine but it's more enlarged than I'd like it to be." (The doctor has an opinion about the inside of my butt!)

Around 10:00 p.m. he calls his wife to the window again and this time he uses the Son of God's full name although we don't know what the "H" stands for. "This is getting crazy," he says as the imaginary ballet music suddenly becomes Pink Floyd. She returns to watch the TV weather to find out the predicted accumulation of these "whitenesses."

With Pink Floyd still being heard, he hears the doctor tell him about "options," each with risks along with a percentage as though he's in Las Vegas with chips in hand pondering his wager. The doctor tells her that, "It's not as bad as we thought but it is serious." (Read that sentence again and then tell me what it means!)

At 6:00 a.m., he's outside shoveling and wearing all the clothes he could rustle on himself but now he doesn't call on the Son of God but instead goes to the Top Guy demanding a curse upon its once beautiful 5:00 p.m. version. His wife is safely inside still watching TV and waiting for the heap's final number. (As though a final number means anything, except proudly announced at her next cocktail party.)

The Pink Floyd music drifts away and Metallica takes over at full volume as he shovels for over an hour and even begins to sweat with sub-zero temperatures. The third person of the Christian Trinity, the Holy Spirit, is never summoned during this experience. Some would say the Holy Spirit is that culprit behind this whiteness.

She decides on chemotherapy and he decides on radiation with both musical sounds playing: lots of ballet ("Hope") with a undercurrent of Metallica ("Oh, well").

The sun comes out the next day and the whiteness becomes grey although "slush" will be its name in a few days.

He brag about his early morning shoveling at work and she gets the final snow total that no one will remember.

The doctor told her that, "You're lucky, we caught it in time and you're fine." The doctor in the next room told him that, "We got this under control but we found some other issues."

"Both Sides Now"

Wanting

*"Bows and flows of angel hair
and ice cream castles in the air
And feather canyons everywhere,
I've looked at clouds that way.
But they only block the sun, they
rain and snow on everyone.
So many things I would have
done but clouds got in my way."*

So begins life's dream. The clouds that open up the sky eventually become barrier clouds. Joni Mitchell paints a complete picture of life. Can we see the open sky again? Can we see it with seven year-old eyes once more?

Illusions

*I've looked at clouds from both sides now,
From up and down, and still somehow
it's cloud illusion I recall, I really don't know clouds at all.*

In our weighing of life we may very well consciously choose illusions over the reality that is too painful to admit. Illusions are always easier to live with?

Illusions, of course, are different than hopes and dreams. We can have all sorts of fanciful thoughts and misconceptions floating around in our heads and hearts. Yet when they surface we can name them for what they are and move on. Dismissing an illusion can be like taking a baseball card out of the bike's spoke. The bike sounds better now and not like a Harley.

Depression

Moons and Junes and Ferris wheels,
the dizzy dancing way you feel
As every fairy tale comes real; I've looked at love that way.
But now it's just another show. you leave 'em laughing when you go
And if you care, don't let them know, don't give yourself away.

We think of depression as a bad thing that needs to be medicated immediately even if you experience diarrhea as a side effect. Depression can be God's gift asking you to wake up after a long sleep; after a long Ferris wheel ride. (Hum Perry Como's "Round and Round"?) Depression can be a faith-reminder that something you've taken for granted is not "for granted" or assumed. Something ruminates within you and it will not let you go. See depression, at least sometimes, as a gift. Open it up and see what's inside. You will be surprised and overwhelmed with the gift that you'll discover within the gift.

Today & Tomorrow

I've looked at love from both sides now,
From give and take, and still somehow,
It's love's illusion I recall. I really don't love at all.
From win and lose, and still somehow,
it's life's illusions I recall, I really don't life at all."

Whenever someone tells you that "I really don't know much about...." you realize that he/she is gaining a lot of knowledge and insight into the topic. With the information pouring in, this person is realizing the wealth of what more information is still out there. This is much better than the person who speaks eloquently and knowledgeably while the entire time you feel a suspicion about the person's knowledge. In other words, it is better to not

 Although Judy Collins had the hit, I think Joni Mitchell's version is more haunting along with her smoky voice. Enjoy.

A Cat's Loving Life

"Sam the Cat" Tells His Story

❝ I stare out the sunny bay window every day and look at the things I'd like to kill but am unable to do so because I live in this house. It's not easy being me.

It's not that I'm unhappy here. It's okay, I guess. But I tell you, that delicious bird flies right past me and I can't help but make that stuttering sound.

My life is quiet for the most part. I'm very hyperactive but you would never guess it from my demeanor. I exhibit to the tall person who also lives here the epitome of royalty. Living here there are no surprises for me. I've seen to that. There is no scent that is foreign to me in this house, no space unknown and I have carefully examined every door. My domain remains secure and comfortable.

Daily Life

If one word could summarize my life it would be comfortable. I make a point of ensuring it. If a stranger other than the tall person enters my domain I will take shelter until a smell can be determined. This may take several visits or several years. It all depends on my mood.

I read somewhere that a dog has an owner and a cat has a butler. I wouldn't have it any other way.

With all this comfort it's still not easy being me. My heart races much faster than the tall person's. Every minute of every day. A simple object on the rug can grab my attention and hold it for a whole twenty-three seconds. I think that's a pretty good attention span. Don't you? You try sleeping 22 1/2 hours a day and see how you feel when you wake up! Sometimes I'll take a nap before going to sleep.

My Time

For eight hours a day I have this little home to myself. This is my time. No strangers, no noise, no tall person; just me during this glorious time. I suspect that the tall person just stands outside the door for eight hours and then re-enters. He doesn't fool me. I know that he's out there but I just pretend that his is, indeed, gone.

I can't seem to keep myself clean. I think that's my plight as a cat. I find myself constantly cleaning myself up. It could be only two minutes ago and I'm back licking and priming myself. The private parts are the most difficult for me to reach. Luckily the tall man has another one of me to take care of that. I appreciate that female presence in my life (although she chases me around the house during the dark hours). And if she sees that I'm sleeping and enjoying myself she'll just jump in to make that spot hers. I guess that happens to people as well.

Fullness of Life

At night just to tease the tall person, I'll jump up and sit on his lap or chest. I then proceed to illustrate to him what total euphoria really is. I spread out and release a slight death sigh and my internal motor softly revs up. If you look up "bliss" in the dictionary, I'm sure you'll see my picture. If he picks me up then it's a, "Oh hum" moment that's not my moment. He'll be watching a movie and I'll unexpectedly jump on him to join him although I have no idea about actors' names nor the movie's plot. He'll pet me one way until I turn my head because it's here that I want a want scratch. No, I was wrong, it's the other ear that needs attention.

And then I thought that I'd show the tall person what it looks like since he will never have it. It's my bliss. It's totally mine and I'm not sharing it. Do I have dreams? I'm not sure but if I did, I'd finally get to kill those things outside.

Mine is not a long life compared to the tall person's but it is mine. When the time comes for me to leave this home he will say, "Thank you" to me before I'm quietly and quickly put to sleep. I don't mind. It's the life of a cat and I've shown the tall person what it's like to be restless and peaceful - all in one day. (And he'll never know about "bliss.")

I Thanked A Teacher

Thankful

On a Saturday afternoon, just for the heck of it, I googled his name to see whether he was alive or dead. After all it's been over 30 years since I had his classes. Lots of names similar to his but then his name showed itself.

Finding him was not as difficult as I thought. I emailed him a simple message and he replied.

Content

There's been teachers over the years for whom I'm still in therapy. But aren't there several or many teachers that stand out for us all? They shine for whatever reason. Presentation, persistence, concern, content?

For me it was content. Neither taking a breath nor pausing he mellifluously filled 50 minutes with beauty, grace and God's love three times a week. It was operatic only without a death at the end.

Those days I would take a half-filled cup of coffee into class and then use the cup as an ashtray while he pronounced theology as I have never heard it before. I couldn't write fast enough. What he shared was everything that you wanted to hear about God's relationship to us but rarely if ever did. He was spouting pure and true theology. Theology of Grace. Nothing could stop this short man from entering the classroom, announcing all these wonderful thoughts as though it was obvious to everyone in the world and then exit at precisely the right moment.

Thank You

My email was simply to thank him for his presentations during the three classes that I took from him. I told him that it has influenced my ministry and my preaching more than he would know. (Perhaps he did already know!)

You may wonder if he remembered me. I wondered that too but then thought that it didn't matter if he remembered me or not. I remember him and what he taught me and how he showed me the best of Catholic theology.

He thanked me and said that my message meant a lot to him. He was still lecturing periodically but now needing a cane. His message to me meant even more than "a lot." His thought provoking lectures continue to provoke thoughts for me in shaping the ministry I enjoy today.

Just Walk Away When A Sentence Begins With ...

"To be honest with you..."

This person has either been lying to you in the past and getting away with it or is about to tell you something that you may not want to hear. It's your choice. (Normally it's the latter.)

"If I were you..."

This magical person is about to transform his/herself into you and decide for you what you haven't decided. (If you allow this person to complete his/her sentence then your car payments ought to be included in the bargain.)

 Psalm 1960."
Enjoy a video I made featuring 1960 songs by a popular artist and set to a made up psalm.

"If you ask me..."

If you keep quiet, let's see if I ask you. (I won't)

"When I was your age..."

A true favorite of those older than ourselves who feel forgotten. So what if they walked three miles to school and ate cold potatoes for lunch. I will not like them any more than I already do.

"Your mother and I both agree that..."

Forget the corporate decision ploy. It was mother who decided and it's your job to dump the bad news on me.

"You hear what I'm saying?"

This sentence occurs often in conversations where the speaker lacks self confidence and apparently has a hearing impairment as well. "I'm standing in front of you, of course I hear you."

"Basically..."

Walk away instantly when someone begins a sentence with "Basically." The suggestion is that this topic is too complicated for your weak mind so the speaker has been kind enough to dumb it down for you.

Trust me. I can handle your complicated story which will take about thirty seconds longer than your "basic" version.

"like" and "awesome" used together way too often

If either word is heard more than once in one sentence then your planets are not in solar with each other because there is nothing "like awesome." "Most unique" anyone?

Advancing Age, Shrinking World

Proportional

What is the greatest hazard about growing old? Besides the arthritis and back pains, the greatest menace in aging is the shrinking of the world. Our world grows smaller as our age increases.

The largeness of a child's world is in direct proportion to her small number of years. "The world is your oyster," the seven-year old is told. "Dream big, and dream hard," the child is constantly told. During those young years there is total mystery and wonder. At each of life's discovery, another new discovery lays before the child. No one day is taken for granted because each new day contains something new or renewing. The smallness of those years holds out the world's wonders.

As the years increase and increase even more, our world tends to shrink. The four bedroom home with a backyard becomes a cozy apartment with a shared backyard. The cozy apartment may soon become an assisted living, smaller apartment with no backyard. The assisted living apartment may soon become a shared room with a stranger and only a curtain dividing the two of you.

And that is only the physical surroundings. Spiritually and mentally, our worlds can also decrease as our age increases. People we have loved have died, our primary focus can rest only ourselves and own personal salvation. The accusation of the "All About Me" generation applies to those in their eighties and nineties as well.

Less Can Mean More

In St. Luke's version of the rich and poor man gospel connects two people. These two characters meet only in the afterlife. Interestingly, in Luke's version the rich man has no name because he is the "Everyman" for the reader. The poor man is named Lazarus because he is a particular, specific person. The wonders and mysteries of their meeting in this life was avoided. Apparently, the two of them have nothing in common, therefore nothing to talk about. How wrong they both are.

The world of that seven year-old girl is enlarged because of its unknown future. The eighty year-old world grows smaller. One older person told me that he knew more dead people than living. So perhaps the worlds of young and old are not that different. One looks forward, the other looks back and cautiously toward the future, or at least the next day. The first has hope and the second, memories. Both worlds contain its own wonder and mystery. Neither can explain either but both relish in its experience - the one "to be" and the one "that was."

The Size of the World Stays the Same

Forget what I said at the beginning. I was wrong to pigeonhole the elderly into small places. The places they inhabit may have shrunk but not their world. The accomplishments of the elderly bring them to this day. We can only hope the seven year-old will find her place someday among the elderly whose world remained wide, open and involving. She's being taught about heaven and the elderly can almost see and taste it. (Whose world is larger now, young one?)

I've heard, "I never thought I'd live this long," as though they had a death age in mind. "Don't get old," is another biggie as though I should buy a gun. "These are supposed to be the 'golden years' when it's full of brass." That one I just smile to. It's just too good to pass up.

Our bodies begin to shrink, bend, feet move slower and often canes and walkers become our new friend. (One person named his, "Scott Walker," Wisconsin's governor whom he did not like.) Our living space decreases, our minds starts to dwindle while all the while these strangers who now have names and histories to share are now our neighbors. They keep the world its proper size. They magnify each other's lives with their widening scopes, differing perspectives and continue to stretch imaginations. These are the folks who keep the wonder and mystery of this life alive and vibrant for us.

The Cross & Two Thieves

Jesus hangs on a cross, a cross that crosses to greater and grander perspectives. Jesus unites two perspectives through and because of his death. The cross becomes not only an object to destroy but also a means to unite. Heaven/Earth, Sin/Grace, Redemption/Judgment.

Evil or shortcomings or weakness or sin or the blind spots in our lives – whatever you wish to call them – can only survive in a vacuum. To stay alive it only needs itself, no oxygen or input. No ventilation to open eyes or hearts. It can only live on its own terms; it's own limited and narrow perspective. That's why as often as "denial" is thrown at us during a personal discussion or argument our evil or sin cannot allow any new information or broadening to be planted in our hearts. It can only live within its own container. Whether we call this newness grace or information it is the process that opens that tightly held lid and breaks the container that keeps us from being more than we are or said spiritually, "blessed by God."

The "unrepentant thief" (no doubt on Jesus' left side, the left always loses) is so boxed in by his beliefs that no graceful air could ever enter his soul. He cannot understand why Jesus isn't doing what he wants to do himself - jump off that cross, kill the Roman soldiers and claim kingship for himself. The other "thief" (he's the one of the "right" side, of course) denounces the lefty guy for missing the whole story, the whole of their lives. He recognizes his weaknesses and appeals to Jesus to make him bigger in the next life than the small life he lived here. His wish is granted by the man who crosses over.

Jesus crosses over and offers both what he's sacrificed. Evil only knows the closed and goodness only knows the possibilities and breath and depth of our lives. No matter the smallest shortcoming or the ugliest of sin, Jesus crosses over and continually invites, urges and prays for us to cross over with him to the greater possibilities of this great gift of life.

Doubting Thomas

Thomas was the one who held out his belief in Him until Jesus appears to him after the resurrection. He's supposed to represent to the rest of us believers who doubt – sometimes or a lot of the times. Yet Thomas does not represent us because he got to touch and feel and to see for himself.

Centuries later we are still doubting and wondering (as well we should) but still looking for that touch, that quick feeling of assurance. If that were to occur in our lives then it would no longer be faith. In fact, it would be fact. "Blessed are those who have not seen and have believed," is how the Thomas story ends. It is the unseen that weighs faith's strength. It is the unknown that measures faith's depth.

A fellow employee was talking to me about beginning a new relationship after an eleven year marriage ended. He said that one night he prayed to God to give him a sign that something was possible for me and the next day he met the woman he's been dating the past three years. So now, he believes. I guess he touched and felt faith. Now he's a lifelong faithful follower of Christ? Time will tell but keep the oxygen flowing through your lungs.

It reminds me of Frank Morgan, the Wizard in "The Wizard of Oz" – with smoke blowing, levers moving up and down, left and right as he maneuvers his omnipotent ways to shock our temporal and fleeting requests. "Ahhh, I guess there is a God," says my confident friend after his supposed divine association.

St. Augustine, writing in 300, summarizes how little time has past between his and our time, how we still forget that we who have not seen are truly blessed, even in our doubts.

Augustine says, "Don't you go drawing back from your God, love your God. You are always saying to him, "Give me this and give me that"…say to him sometimes…"Give me yourself."

If you love him, love him for nothing… don't be a shameless fool. You would not be pleased with your wife if she loved your gold…if the reason she loved you was that you had given her gold or given her a fine dress or given her a splendid villa or given her a special slave or given her a handsome eunuch because if these were the things she loved about you, she would be loving you.

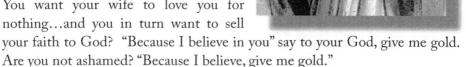

Don't rejoice in such love as that, the adulterer very often can give more.
You want your wife to love you for nothing…and you in turn want to sell your faith to God? "Because I believe in you" say to your God, give me gold. Are you not ashamed? "Because I believe, give me gold."

 You have put your faith up for auction. Notice its price. that is not what it is worth…it is not to be valued in gold or silver…that is not what your faith is worth.

It has a huge price tag; God himself is its price…love him and love him freely for nothing. You see, if you love him on account of something else you aren't loving him at all.

You must not want him for the sake of anything else but whatever else you want you must love for his sake, so that everything else may be referred to love of him, not so that he may be referred to other loves, but that he may be preferred to other loves.

Love him, love him freely… for nothing.

"There's that silver pen that I haven't used for quite a while. I thought I put it in that drawer but I must have moved it."

A note. Thoughts shared between two people with no other audience. A note. Handwritten to make words have meaning. A note. Saved and savored, some forever.

"Oh, the pen was right were I left it on the shelf. Now, where's all that stationary that I've been saving and haven't used for years. Good, there it is. Let's see, how do I begin."

A phone's text message gives the facts, Twitter has a limit with no feeling, Instagram eludes me and an email fails to convey something more. "Facebook," just forget about it.

Ummm, where to start, where to begin. It's just a 'thank you' note but I want to convey how much I felt about our time together. 'Hi,' 'Greetings,' 'Dear,' all seem to be ambiguous and vague. Well, I like 'Dear' for its proper beginning. Oh goodness, look at my handwriting after years of computer typing. I can barely read it, how am I to expect my friend to enjoy this handwritten note. Oh, it doesn't matter because this is authentic."

Telephone calls are still in operation, you can always "leave a message after the beep or stay on the line for other options." (What other options are there?!) You can also assume your gratitude toward the enjoyable evening with your friend and hope that she enjoyed it as well. You can also talk about the previous enjoyable evenings during the next unplanned enjoyable evening with your friend in an unknown future. (After all, we're all going to live forever.)

"Just look at my sentences, they all run uphill. When did I start to write this way? Since I'm left-handed, some of the ink stays on my fingers and runs through the previous words. Oh my, how did people do this years ago?"

There, I'm finished. I can't proof read or correct it because it's down there in all its glorious and dried ink. It is forever written and preserved for my recipient.

My email was sent and I received a reply an hour ago and I'm now watching a comedy show on TV and reading the news on my laptop. I'm glad I sent that handwritten letter to my good friend. (Notice, it's not a message or any other word but it is a letter.)

"I need to carefully fold the letter and place it in an envelope. I hate when the creases don't match. I left an envelope here somewhere, oh, there it is. I'll lick it closed and carefully write the address on the front of the envelope along with my return address in case it needs to be returned to me after its days-long flight toward its destination. Oh, that's right! The stamp! I wonder what stamps cost these days. I'll do that tomorrow. I hope she likes it, it's my monogram in dark colors against a cream stationary. I said everything that I wanted to say about our evening together. I hope she receives it and likes it. Oh wow. Did I sign the letter? I already sealed the envelope. I'm sure that I'm not sure that I signed it. And I was even there when I was writing it. I'm sure of it. It is finished."

So, what is saved forever and what is deleted? (Delete, a word we never used before computers.) What holds and endures our attention and what is dismissed in the midst of what is so dismissible?

A lost art or just a loving art that's been misplaced...at least for the moment?

She opened the letter two days later and carefully read it, twice. She placed it on top of other handwritten letters that meant a lot to her.

They planned on another dinner in two weeks - via email, oh well.

One, Tiny Flame

There it is, now lit. It took longer to light this time because the wick is lower and I just can't seem to reach deep enough inside to relight it. But I did.

The house is still heated, I can't rely on that little flame to flame forth a comfortable, warm winter home. Heck, if I quickly stood up right now I think it'd go out. Oh wait. Forget that. I just tried it and it didn't go out   this little, small flame on my kitchen table with a supposed spruce scent that "fills the room" as the box falsely stated. I didn't buy the candle for

the scent but for the small flame, although a nice scent would have been be
ıiıı ı.

It flickers, ever so slowly as it tries to keep itself alive. The heating wax surrounding it allows the tiny flame to stay lit. Is it enough to turn off the kitchen light? I'm not even trying because it's a silly question. If it can't heat then it certainly can't illuminate.

I like the teeny flame because it seems to show everything when it barely shows anything. If folks walked into my kitchen now they would not say, "Oh, what a beautiful flame you have going here." It wouldn't be noticed. It would remain an unsaid piece in the room. None would smell the scent as the box described and our conversation would move to topics that interest them.

But they're not here. It is just me and a single, miniature version of those real flames that surround a veterans memorial or a park's statue. My tiny flame doesn't mark great or grand events but only the passing thoughts that pass my mind as quickly as they enter. Random, varied; none solved or resolved. Perhaps a few reenactments of a personal play that cannot be replayed run through my mind but it seems productive even if the reproduction turns out the same way. It's my single flame. I can have an opening and closing night in one hour if I want to.

I considered a larger candle, hence a larger flame but thought, "Why?" as I stare at my small version.

Wax builds up as the flame continues which can pose problems for this tiny thing that neither brightens or scents as the box promised. The surrounding wax can keep the tiny flame vibrant and alive but the same wax can also drown the flame. Without careful observation on my part the wax may extinguish my undersized flame. Interesting how the needed wax can also become its drowning wax. I need to keep the minute flame lit every minute I observe it.

One flame. No scent in spite of the box's description. No one around now to comment, criticize, weigh or measure my kitchen flame or my momentary thoughts. I'm watching the heat-filled wax build up now so it doesn't triumph.

It's my night. It is my single flame. I don't mind that I miss the scent which the box assured. It's my flame. And I enjoy it every single night or is this its last night.

_____Key_____

Single Flame: the pilot light of our lives that keeps burning through all times of life.

Scent: the promises of life are not always realized, real or imagined.

Wax: those who support and encourage us keep the flame alive and those who intrude and want to make us like themselves overwhelms the single flame.

Re-enactments: upon reflection we try to reshape made-decisions, unmade-decisions, missed opportunities and opportunities that went sour as though enacting them again will change the result.

Single flame: what gets us out of bed in the morning and lights our day ahead and allowing for a good night's sleep to prepare us for the next day.

Walter, My Dad

Dutifully went to work at the newly formed credit union for over 40 years. That adverb cannot be emphasized enough. 8-5 and Fridays until 8 pm were the hours he kept while continually warning clients that a credit union is not a bank but a safe place to invest their money. He was its manager begun with a small group of investors who all gave $1.00 except my dad, because as he said later, "I wasn't sure it would make it."

At 46 years-old, my friends would ask me, "How's your grandfather?" not knowing there's three siblings before me and one after.

He wanted to take the car to work but my mother insisted that he should walk for the exercise, a simple 30 minute walk. I long to hear his thoughts as he made his way to work.

A secretary and my dad comprised the early days of credit unions. A simple call from home with the extension "395 please" connected us with this silent, tall man with a gentle smile. "Mom wanted us to call if you'd be home for supper," asked the grandson/son and he'd say, "You kids go ahead without me."

Today's TV version of my dad's late nights would have him cooped up in the local motel with his secretary or at our hometown Manitowoc, "Warren's Restaurant's" waitress or selling drugs on its main street, Washington, to help pay the bills or worse yet in a van in a hit TV series making drugs for the already drugged-from-the-small-ghetto-town kids that Manitowoc produced. (See "Breaking Bad" for the last reference.)

The fireplace was his "man cave" as we call it today except it was built to extend our kitchen. There he'd sit with his cigar and a glowing fireplace flame, one less than the other. I wonder today what thoughts he had as he exhaled the cigar smoke with his stolid stare outside our kitchen window. To interrupt him during those hours was always surprising to him - and to me. He'd answer the kid's question and then return to his stare. (As years wore on he'd sometimes mistaken my name for our dead cat but that's beside the point.)

Born in 1906 adding to the number of a small day care center today, Walter finished high school and enrolled in a seminary in the big city of Milwaukee in the 1920's only to leave the seminary and return to begin this new business.

No one knows today why he left. He loved his retirement as much as he loved his work, over thirty years of retirement. My mother, the outgoing parent, passed away first and my dad's final eight years were spent with the five of us kids.

He stilled smoked cheap cigars and still stared out the new window from his new home. Our neighboring hospital wished to expand its parking lot (small town, remember? Parking problem?) and thirteen homes were relocated through Habitat for Humanity. My dad was the last to sell his house in this growing non-metropolis. The hospital's finance director visits him along with my sister and me.

His cigars and staring may have paid off. The hospital guy offers top dollar for Walter's house. He likes that but asks for another home - rent free for the rest of his life. The hospital guy smiles and says, "yes." My dad adds, "snow, grass removal included." Hospital guy smirks and says, "Yes." I told my dad, "What about cable?" and he looked at me to keep my mouth shut. "Washer and dryer," my dad returns with and the hospital guy again gives in. The papers are placed before him, he signs them and says "I like that pen." Hospital guy then ... well you know what he did.

I was never into sports but playing with my aging dad would have meant disaster if I'd hit him in the head with his arms folded in front of me wondering what the two of us were doing. Didn't happen. But he did listen.

Rarely, if ever, responded but he listened to all the stories we kids were willing to tell him. Some sordid and others just about growing up. He sat there and listened. absorbing and absorbed by all the information. The squeeze to let out an opinion after all that absorbing? Never happened.

My dad. He worked very well, he wanted to be priest for some reason, marries giving five children not knowing what to do with them nor always knowing their names, retires well and dies peacefully at 93. His squeeze?

The five of us are still waiting.

The Mother of My Invention

She was late. An important day for me and the Church. You're only ordained once in a lifetime and she decides to take a walk around the block with a  priest friend. They must have walked slowly. The choir was ready, everyone sat silently as the 5 o'clock bells rang. She's not in sight or standing next to my dad for the entrance procession. The retired bishop whispers, "Where's the mother?" and priests shrugged their shoulders. Long minutes pass and she arrives telling me that they "got talking." The opening song begins, they all stand, the ceremony begins and the task is accomplished complete with prostration and oiled hands. It all worked out.

Mother. Doesn't it always always work out? Hardly, when you multiple biological mom with life's other "moms" you've either created or learned. There's the mom of the earth whose nature appears to have destined you toward a fixed purpose. There's the mother of entitlement to take advantage of whatever society offers or is available to you. There's life's motherlode when all appears to others to fall together for you which only creates envy and jealous. There's the self-nourishing mother you've earned only through many years of practice. There's the mother you attempt to substitute for the biological one which now gives you someone to blame when you don't get what you want.

Mothers surround our lives daily. Being able to recognize and name her each time may help and assist us in our journey of self discovery.

She wasn't late that day. Mother was present all the time for the opening song. I just didn't know which mother it was.

Perfection? You're Kidding...or Not?

"It was a perfect evening." "That dress fits you perfectly," (yeah, just wait a year), "This school is perfect for you," "The boss is coming over tonight, everything needs to be perfect!" and the best of all, "I'm perfectly content being alone."

Like "absolutely," "basically" and "honestly," another word can be added to our list of exaggerations, "perfect."

What may have been "perfect" at your wedding is that the troublesome guy didn't show up. "She's the picture of perfection," says the guy who wants to frame and hang the object of his affection who happens to be human.

Does perfect mean there's no mistakes or mishaps as inevitably occurs in life? If that's true, it's like saying, "If you're not sick, you must be very healthy!"

Perfection is reached when mistakes are acknowledged and most importantly smiled upon by two people. (Now there's a wedding card.)

The perfection of Jesus is overrated when quick examples are provided; denying his mother more wine, scoffing at the woman who asked him for something and comparing her to dogs and doubting God at Gethsemane when he bargains God to pass the cup pass him. So, wasn't Jesus perfect in his imperfections? Is the miracle of the carpenter's-son made-God that he was able to learn from mistakes and move just a tad closer to "who he is"- the same challenge that is given us every day of our lives?

Beginning your day with hopes of perfection just swallows that same day into life's twists. (Maybe it's a Midwest thing where every sunny day has the remark, "Oh, but it'll rain tomorrow!") I don't know but I think a type of perfection is achievable through mistakes.

We know everything that I'm saying but we hope to trick those around us into thinking that we've achieved it. They smile and envy us while walking away jealous. (The games we play with each other.)

If I were in architecture, I guess it'd be a different game with lots of checks and rechecks. But this is my human life, complete with all its imperfections.

Raising five children, as though a single parent, was difficult for my mother. My silent dad was more silent during these times. My mother was the complete parent - coach, disciplinarian, comforter and solverer of all our petty children problems. I forgot to mention head chef, even though I'm told cooking was not an easy task for her.

She had her emotional problems that we children labeled her by. It was that label or this label attached to her that allowed us to rise above her - in her mistakes and mishaps. But her job was always done - oatmeal for students off to school and a hearty meal in the evenings with homework completed before bed. Her encouragement of us all was boundless but we sensed something missing inside herself, her personal life.

Only as adults would it be clear to us. For years I carried her imperfections as my definition of her. It was convenient and comfortable to contain her that way. Years after her death it finally hit me - my mother was perfect in her imperfections. She performed all of it for us growing kids in spite of what held her down emotionally.

For some reason, a friend told me about a moving symphony that I might enjoy. I made playing the symphony my Good Friday ritual after our congregation's service. And one year while hearing it, her perfection hit me headstrong. It became clear that my assumptions and presumptions of her were both inaccurate and a false judgment of her life. I cannot tell her now but I hope she hears the symphony as I now hear it every Good Friday. My mother was perfect in her imperfections. Is "in spite of" or "because of?" I choose the latter.

I like making mistakes. It gives others an opportunity to correct me which makes them feel good about themselves and also helps me. I'm learning that it's better to serve the better wine when the lesser was served first, it's listening to the woman kneeling before me with her simple request and the great Gethsemane of acceptance is the God-path I need to follow and I'm learning how a simple woman/mother tried her best to raise five children.

It is perfect? Or, is it perfectly done in all my imperfections?

My "Good Friday,"symphony
Henryk Gorecki, Symphony No.3, Op.36
(Symphony of Sorrowful Songs)

Rembert G. Weakland, OSB.

by Todd Robert Murphy

The brick pavers surrounding the Eiffel Tower were made in the small town of Patton, Pa. The city of Patton was at one time the largest manufacturer of bricks in the world. A young novitiate from Patton would walk on his hometown pavers many times throughout his life. He would make his solemn profession as a Benedictine monk a little more than an hour away from post-war Paris in 1949 at the Solesmes Benedictine Abbey. He would take the name Rembert.

That was the beginning of a long and circuitous road for this future prelate of the Roman Catholic Church, Rembert Weakland. His passage would be flecked with accomplishment, controversy, disappointment and self-doubt. There would be times of great exhilaration, deep despair and loneliness. But one thing was indisputable from the very beginning: Weakland was a very gifted and holy man with a shining future in the Roman Catholic Church.

In 1977, Pope Paul VI elevated Weakland to archbishop of Milwaukee. At the time, many of the Catholic faithful were confused by the choice of Weakland, given his reputation as a church intellectual. Most thought it would be a only few years before he was given a red cap signifying him a cardinal of the church and moved on. That might have been in the back of his mind, too.

He was a cultural misfit in Milwaukee, and in his early tenure he was seen as a bit aloof by some. The Milwaukee Archdiocese, for lack of a better description, is a blue-collar, conservative Catholic community, and he was a progressive in the church. In his 2009 biography, he acknowledged his lack of comfort and feeling of isolation when he relocated to a town best known for beer, bowling and the TV show "Laverne & Shirley."

the church needed to evolve after Vatican II.

His views were consistent with most American Catholics. Weakland believed that to stay relevant with the faithful, the church needed to evolve after Vatican II. The issues facing the American church were not yet germane to Catholics in other parts of the world. The perplexity was to evolve but to stay one with the worldwide Catholic community and the Vatican, a difficult balance to achieve.

Cardinal Joseph Bernardin of Chicago was an ally, but Weakland's voice in the church soon would be cut short with the death of Pope Paul VI. The decades-long leadership of the more conservative Pope John Paul II changed the welcome mat message for his voice in the Vatican. Weakland and the Holy See didn't always have a harmonious relationship, so he began to use his pulpit as a bully pulpit to address the issues confronting a restless American faithful.

It wasn't that Weakland's views were controversial in most American dioceses, but rather that the Holy See moved at a slower pace. Weakland felt an urgency that was not shared or endorsed by the Vatican. These were the issues many American Catholic families were dealing with daily. Rome's strategy was avoidance. The Holy See's attitude was the intellectual equivalent to former first lady Nancy Reagan telling people to "just say no" to drugs. American life was a bit more complicated than a simple admonition and exercise of willpower.

Weakland took it upon himself to address issues such as abortion, greater roles for women in the church, social and economic justice, homosexuality, AIDS, sex education, clerical pedophilia and feminism. He acknowledged that a person could, perhaps, reconcile his or her pro-choice views and still be a good Catholic. Or that he would consider ordaining a married man, who was worthy, into the priesthood because of a shortage of priests. He wanted expanded roles for women in the church and held out the possibility of ordination of women when the Vatican was still opposed to children serving as altar girls alongside altar boys. The innocuous little things he endured, such as criticisms about the use of altar girls, made no sense to most American Catholics. And he held out the possibility that ordaining women might lead to "a more intelligent and compassionate church."

he came to accept that his voice would conflict with the Curia in Rome

Weakland always disliked being typecast as a liberal or conservative, but over the years he came to accept that his voice would conflict at times with the Curia in Rome. The church's hierarchy was more in tune with the doctrinal orthodoxy, and he would be cast as a more liberal voice in the church. He would ostracize the tactics of the pro-life movements and then was labeled pro-choice, which he is not. After celebrating a "Respect Life" Mass, he was pilloried for commenting afterward: "Such a difficult group to preach to," "Such hard faces," "Such surety," "No smiles," "No openness to any other point of view. They have no joy in being Catholic or part of a church." He went on to say that many dislike the narrowness, lack of compassion and lack of civility of the pro-life movement.

The archbishop's renovation of the Cathedral of St. John the Evangelist (my parish) was also subjected to unfair criticism. His detractors finally had a symbolic but tangible issue to voice objection. The real motivator was the archbishop's past pronouncements on topics on which they disagreed with him. But now the critics had what they considered an abomination of a renovated cathedral so they all could join in and scorn his destructive ways. It backfired.

It was during that time that Weakland sought my help with the naysayers, and I gladly provided it. His fault-finders called it a pagan temple, but upon its completion few people argue with the restored magnificence of the cathedral. In the years since its completion, I've yet to meet anyone who hasn't commented on its beauty.

Weakland's personal issues came to light in May 2002, when he paid off a male lover on the advice of legal counsel. Weakland also came out of the closet. And we learned that he followed established protocol of moving sexually abusive priests to other parishes once a psychological exam was completed. He acknowledged that he, like many of his brethren, was wrong to do so and asked for forgiveness. Many have concluded that there will never be, nor can there be, closure for those who have been abused by a priest regardless of compensation, apologies and pleas for forgiveness. And maybe that's the church's cross to bear.

The crowded Saturday evening Mass at St. John a few days after Weakland's transgressions were made public was filled with people whose expressions went from disbelief, betrayal and sadness to even anger. Father Mike said Mass and spoke briefly about what we all knew to be true: Our archbishop had sinned, and it was a whopper as sins go. People cried, parishioners hugged each other and strangers lined the back of the cathedral in tears; the sadness was palpable. It was a career-ending blow to the archbishop, and he quickly retired.

In truth, Milwaukee has blundered by not turning to Weakland's sagacious counsel in many circumstances in which he could have provided guidance. We seem to have exiled him. Is it because we are uncomfortable with the sin — or the sinner?

The archbishop's sins should be treated with empathy and forgiveness; he, like all of us, is a fallible person. You see when you cut through all the doctrine and church politics that being Catholic with a capital C is about forgiveness. It's really not any more complicated than that one word. God's forgiveness is greater than any sin any of us can commit.

The societal matters that Weakland was at the forefront of addressing 25 years ago are the same issues and questions that Pope Francis has been raising during the past 16 months.

Archbishop Rembert Weakland, OSB
autobiography, "A Pilgrim in a Pilgrim Church"

Who Are You When You're No Longer Who You Were?

It was the neatly carved out segments that created your day for over forty years. Each segment of time had a purpose and when one ended the next one began.

Then came the preverbal "gold watch" and suddenly Monday morning begins and you discover that the whole day becomes a segment. Filling it seems impossible following the comfort of the previous experience.

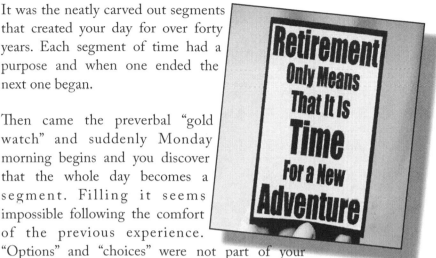

"Options" and "choices" were not part of your vocabulary during those years but now they haunt you from the moment you get out of bed, whatever time that may be.

Who you were then was that job that consumed energy and interests – perhaps even sleepless nights with a morning decision needed or deadlines that were almost missed. The familiar and new faces over the many years, the tasks and duties that provided for your family are gone when you left that last day with a box containing your family picture, paper clips and the company stapler (we should always take a little something when we leave, don't you think?).

9:00 a.m. on the morning you've been waiting for, for all those long years has arrived. It's cloudy with a chance of rain and you believe that to be true about yourself as well. Options and choices continue to ring in your ears. A slow breakfast is your first thought and wondering if you'll create a new pattern of daily breakfasts like that. Volunteering for that favorite charity comes to mind but then slowly seems to dwindle as the hours seem longer now than they did while you were working. "The Price is Right" is on now but watching crazy people jump up and down in your bathrobe just doesn't seem right. "There's golf," but at your age if you didn't play it before then you will not play it now.

At parties or gatherings how long does it take before the most important question is asked of you or you ask it to someone, "So, what do you do?" Identity is then connected by the occupation that occupied your segments for all those years. Saying you're "retired" moves the person to the next person. Or, "Oh, you're lucky," says the person wondering if she'll watch "The Price is Right" a few years from now. Or, worst yet, "What **did** you do for a living." (We're going to identify you by your work if it's the last thing we do!)

A friend gave me one of the best lines for life, "You are in old age as you've always been, only more so." The "were" that distracts you now is answered by the same question a teenager asks, "Who are you?" "Were" looks back at a time that no longer exists and is over. "Who" is always the question that is never quite completely answered but clues are provided, like a treasure hunt, throughout our long lives.

You slowly forget the "gold watch" that you didn't really receive and look for the "gold" that is always before you. It is the "who" that you've always been and will continue to be. The interesting part of my friend's quote is the "more so." How can you fill these new segments of your life with "more so" of yourself?

"Walking With Jesus"

That's what a church sign shows me driving to work. I thought how difficult that is for us. I don't mean the usual stuff of sacrifice or dedication. I mean it's difficult because we know how his story ends. It's not fair walking with someone when you know how the something of his life turns out.

I'm at an age where the first few words of hearing the gospel, I say to myself, "Oh, it's that one again" and my mind wanders toward lunch. I'm able to do the same thing with songs of my era, four notes into it is my best and I can tell you the artist, title and sometimes the record label. (Church repetition and radio days do have some things in common.)

Traditional piety is in knowing the end of Jesus' story in order for us to copy it as best as possible. Isn't it more enriching and rewarding to question Jesus along side along with those doubting apostles we hear about on Sunday? If you notice, after the resurrection Jesus tells his disciples the good stuff when no one else is around. (Ohhh, I just wrecked it for many of you...now you know that he resurrects. Darn it.) Can we identify with any of those biblical needy folks who approached Jesus looking for something but not knowing if he's able to help? My favorite Biblical story is the blind guy who approaches Jesus for a cure and Jesus asks the most  profound question to him: "What do you want?" Isn't it obvious? But it is not obvious until the seeker knows what to seek.

All the Jesus movies are viewed with its sensational ending waiting in our minds. Scourging, thorns or the final spear, we know what happens next. He comes back to life, scares the guys with his "peace to you" statements, eats a lot of fish, ascends up and away and sends the Holy Spirit while he assumes his position at the right hand of his rightful position (which he already possessed since the beginning.)

I want to walk with Jesus. I'd love to have him along side of me. Sometimes I wish that I didn't know his ending so that our walk together might be a truly mutual walk with surprises along the way along with unknown endings.

It's the Journey Not the Destination

Colonel Potter on "M.A.S.H." gave a line that I've never forgotten, "If you aren't where you are then you are no where." With that, the conversation between Hawkeye and him ended

So much of religion is concerned with preparing ourselves for some place we know nothing about, heaven. Oh yes, we can speculate and postulate until we're blue (or purple) but at the end of the book or lecture we are still left with this inevitable end to our lives and this "some place" of a destination that follows. (Actually, loosely used, heaven is only after the second coming of Christ. In the meantime graves are visited by family and friends twice a year to change the flowers.)

Unfortunately the unknown and vague destination provides excellent fodder for anyone, anywhere to say anything about heaven's pathway and then pass a collection basket to compliment the speaker on speculating better than others have on something the speaker has no personal knowledge of, yet spoke eloquently about. (Is religion great or what?)

Focusing on the journey rather than the destination tasks us with more immediate concerns because the journey focuses on today and the day after the next. This is where I have a degree of control and influence. It is here that my life is lived and presumably pathed toward hopefully the upper part of my eternal resting place. If we could only cease with destination talk and focus on journey themes then something exciting and life-giving certainly occurs.

Terrorists are promised a special place in eternal life for their misguided "sacrifices." I'm always surprised more Catholics don't commit suicide because of the next life's bliss. (I guess making suicide a mortal sin delays our eternal delight so we just need to keep soldiering onward.)

How we constantly miss the point of the person in front of us baffles me.

The person in front of us in this life wishes for a listening ear, a genuine smile and attentive eyes. We spare a moment and we listen. We smile or grimace depending on the nature of the story. We wish the person well and promise a remembrance in our prayers. There is no reward or merit. It is this journey, not that destination that is lived and celebrated during that brief moment and, by the way, every time we gather for the Eucharist.

The new Mass prayers of the Catholic Church has the word "merit" pop up a lot; way too much, for my theological tastes. It is heresy, as I remember which places our deeds, prayers or actions to somehow cause that "unknown" place to some day be ours.

Nothing can get us to our final destination earned or rewarded. Heaven is not granted on a point system or number of hosts eaten or rosaries said. The Psalms tell us that "sacrifice and burnt offerings" is not what God wants but a "contrite heart." I think Catholics have a more difficult time with this thinking than other Christian religions because we somehow were taught that heaven is a place that is worked toward, earned. The destination can never be achieved because of our accumulative actions and deeds. That's why the old joke about those who ate meat on Fridays are now in hell is a senseless belief because that's not the salvation Jesus won (earned) for us.

What we all do know, what we all cherish and what we all appreciate is this life that we've been graced with - this day and hopefully for several more tomorrows. What comes after, "Who really cares?" Can't we give God at least something to do? After all, He is God!

I began with the fictional character Colonel Potter so I close with another fictional character, Jiminy Cricket, "Be good for goodness sake."

"Be good for goodness sake."

45579815R00058

Made in the USA
San Bernardino, CA
11 February 2017